David,

Great to meet you and enjoy your work. thanks for being part of the Koby Mandell Foundation

Seth + Sherri Mandell

JERUSALEM
Published by
ORTHODOX UNION
תורה ומצוות
U
NCSY
Produced by
Mesorah Publications, ltd

the eye of the universe

A Pictorial Tour of the Holy City

TEXT BY

RABBI ARYEH KAPLAN

Illustration Credits

Avrohom Biderman, Brooklyn: pp. 48-bottom, 108

Igor German Foto-Works, Jerusalem: pp. 9, 11, 20, 31, 53, 54

Yeshara Gold, Jerusalem: pp. 17, 27, 29, 30-top, 32, 33, 34, 35, 36, 37, 38, 40, 41, 43, 44, 48-top, 55, 56, 59, 60, 62, 66, 67, 68, 74-bottom, 75, 76, 78, 79, 80, 81, 82, 84, 85, 86, 88, 97, 103, 104, 105, 106, 109, 110, 111, 112, 113, 121, 122, 123, 124, 128, 130, 131, 132, 133, 134-bottom, 135,146, 152

From the private collection of Rabbi M. Hus, Jerusalem: pp. 14, 15, 18, 19, 22, 23, 24-top, 38, 39, 42, 60, 70

Eli Kroen, Brooklyn: pp. 8, 16-top, 37, 45 , 49, 51-center and bottom, 58, 63, 69, 74, 77, 87, 89, 100, 102, 126, 127, 136, 137, 138, 139, 140, 144, 145

Shmuel and Pearl Margereten, Monsey: pp. 24-bottom, 46, 50, 57, 69, 72, 90, 115

Orthodox Union / NCSY: p. 151

With permission of Palphot, Ltd., Haifa: pp. 12-13, 16-bottom, 25, 26, 28, 30-bottom, 51-top, 52, 71, 83, 99, 134-top, 141, 145, 147, 148, 150, 153

Naomi Roth, Brooklyn: p. 127

Eliyahu Saftlas, Brooklyn: pp. 21, 91, 107, 118, 119, 120, 129

Yitzchok Saftlas/Bottom Line Design, Brooklyn: pp. 94, 96, 98, 101, 114, 125, 143

Irving Schild, New York City, © *1996, Irving Schild:* pp. 10, 47, 65, 73, 92, 93, 95, 117, 142, 149

Fraidy Shuster, Brooklyn: p. 116

First edition – First impression / August 1996

Published by the NATIONAL CONFERENCE OF SYNAGOGUE YOUTH/
UNION OF ORTHODOX JEWISH CONGREGATIONS OF AMERICA
333 Seventh Avenue / New York, N.Y 10001 / (212) 563-4000

Produced and Distributed by MESORAH PUBLICATIONS, LTD.
4401 Second Avenue / Brooklyn, N.Y 11232 / (718) 921-9000

Distributed in Israel by SIFRIATI / A. GITLER
4 Bilu Street / P.O.B. 14075 / Tel Aviv 61140

Distributed in Europe by J. LEHMANN HEBREW BOOKSELLERS
20 Cambridge Terrace / Gateshead, Tyne and Wear / England NE8 1RP

Distributed in Australia and New Zealand by GOLDS BOOK & GIFT SHOP
36 William Street / Balaclava 3183, Vic., Australia

Distributed in South Africa by KOLLEL BOOKSHOP
22 Muller Street / Yeoville 2198, Johannesburg, South Africa

ISBN: 0-89906-588-0

Graphic design, photo enhancement, and color separations
by Eli Kroen at ArtScroll Studios, Brooklyn, N.Y.

Printed in the United States of America
by Edison Lithographing and Printing Corp. / North Bergen, N.J.

Custom bound by Sefercraft, Inc. / 4401 Second Avenue / Brooklyn N.Y. 11232

וראה בטוב ירושלים כל ימי חייך
וראה בנים לבניך שלום על ישראל

May you gaze upon the goodness of Jerusalem, all the days of your life.
And may you see children born to your children, peace upon Israel. (Psalms 128:6-7)

Dedicated to the memory of

שמואל ב״ר יששכר דוב ז״ל — **Sam Teichman** ז״ל

ליבה ברײנדל בת ר׳ יהושע הלוי ע״ה — **Lujda Teichman** ע״ה

רחל בת ר׳ אלכסנדר סנדר ע״ה — **Rose Teichman** ע״ה

יצחק אײזיק ב״ר אברהם חיים ז״ל — **Isaac Nae** ז״ל

They taught us to recognize that
what is holy is good,
and they left us an eternal legacy
of dedication to the Torah as our way of life.

תנצב״ה

Contents

Preface

by Rabbi Pinchas Stolper

Jerusalem evokes emotion and concern in the heart and mind of every human being. It has become the concern of many nations. Why? Is it not that the first human beings Adam and Eve were created from the dust of the Altar of the Holy Temple? If so, each and every human being is made of the very dust of G-d's Temple — indeed the Eye of the Universe.

The story is told that the sainted Chofetz Chaim received a letter from a Jewish soldier who was drafted into the Polish army. The soldier related that he was assigned to a remote base where there were no Jewish soldiers, no minyan, no facilities for kashruth and where it was impossible to keep Shabbos. His question: "How do I survive as an observant Jew?"

The reply of the Chofetz Chaim is awesome: "If it is impossible for you to keep Shabbos, kashruth, to daven or to keep mitzvos, don't be discouraged. But there is one thing you must do. Whenever you have a moment, speak to G-d, and whenever you speak to G-d, face east.

"Why face east? Because you will be directing your thoughts to Jerusalem and in so doing you will unite yourself with the Jewish people and with G-d. In effect, whenever a Jew faces Jerusalem in prayer — he *is* in Jerusalem."

For the world at large the history of Jerusalem opens with its conquest by King David. For the Jew, Jerusalem is the place where man was created. Jerusalem is the city of Malkizedek, the city in which Abraham and Jacob worshiped, the city chosen by G-d, whose mission is to radiate direction and spirituality to all mankind.

What is the source of Jerusalem's uniqueness? Why is it the only city mentioned in our prayers? What is the source of its holiness, the mystery of its origin? Why can G-d's Temple be located on this spot and nowhere else? How are Adam, Eve, Cain and Abel connected with Jerusalem? Why is Jerusalem's status and destiny of such deep concern to scores of nations around the globe and to Judaism's daughter religions? Why is the Temple of such momentous significance? Why does the Jew feel that a world without the Jerusalem Temple is a world destroyed and desolate? If you visit Jerusalem today you will be moved by its beauty, its expanse, its bustling population, its thousands of Torah scholars and scores of Yeshivot. Why then do we *still* mourn over its destruction?

Why, during the past two thousand years, have Jews prayed, "Blessed are You, Eternal G-d, Who is building Jerusalem" — in the present tense — while Jerusalem lay destroyed and desolate?

Rabbi Kaplan's book insightfully contains the answers to these questions. Jerusalem is at the heart of the Jewish experience; it is literally the Eye of the Universe, because it is the one spot on earth where the presence of G-d is most evident and most concentrated. It is from Jerusalem that human fulfillment and redemption will come.

JAFFA GATE
ميدان عمر بن الخطاب
OMAR IBN-EL-KHATTAB SQ.
שאלו שלום
THE PEACE OF JERUSALEM
THE GATE

Introduction

Opposite: *We enter the Old City through the Jaffa Gate.*

Below: *One of the Old City's countless arched alleys built on the slopes of the Judean hills*

Two holy days are observed by virtually every Jew: Yom Kippur and Passover, two of the most significant days of the Jewish calendar.

The most dramatic part of the Yom Kippur service occurs at the close of the day, just as the service is about to end. To announce the conclusion of this most sacred day, a long clear blast is sounded on the *shofar*. The congregation responds, "Next year in Jerusalem!"

At the conclusion of every Jewish wedding ceremony, it is customary for the groom to break a glass.[1] Among Ashkenazic (Northern European) Jews, the custom is to shout *Mazel Tov* at this point. But Sefardic (Southern European) Jews recite the verse, "If I forget you, O Jerusalem, let my right hand forget its cunning" (Psalms 137:5).

The glass is broken so that even at the happiest moment of their lives, the bride and groom should recall the destruction of

At every hour of the day, the Kotel Hamaaravi, or Western Wall, is a magnet for Jews pouring out their hearts in prayer, or seeking to touch our past. Beyond the Wall once stood the Temple, and that is where it will stand again, may it happen speedily, in our days, amen.

Jerusalem. This is in keeping with the next verse, "Let my tongue stick to my palate if I remember you not, if I set not Jerusalem above my greatest joy" (ibid. 137:6).

Every synagogue in the world is built facing Jerusalem. Since both Europe and the United States are west of Jerusalem, their synagogues were traditionally built facing east. But in any part of the world, when a synagogue is built, it always faces Jerusalem. Thus, whenever a Jew prays, he faces this Holy City.

But what is the significance of Jerusalem? Why should this one city be so all-important to the Jewish people? What makes it unique?

In the following pages, we shall explore some of these questions and attempt to understand just what Jerusalem is.

Beginnings

A portal to history — the timeless stones of the timeless city tell the story of centuries.

It is significant to note that Jerusalem is never actually mentioned in the Torah, although there are many allusions to it. When the Torah speaks of Jerusalem, it always uses such terms as "the place that God will choose," or "the place that God will choose to make His Name dwell there."[1]

Rambam *(Maimonides)* states that there are three reasons why the Torah does not explicitly name the place that would be chosen by God. First, if the nations had learned that this place was destined to be the center of the highest religious ideals, they would have occupied it and prevented the Jews from ever controlling it, even as many nations attempt to do today. Second, the tribes in possession of Jerusalem might have destroyed it; or, knowing of its spiritual importance, might have made it a center of idolatry. Third, and possibly most important, each one of the twelve tribes of Israel would have desired to

A panoramic view of Jerusalem. In the foreground is the ancient wall around the Temple complex. In the background is the bustling, fast growing New City, whose skyline is dotted with tall luxury hotels.

have this city within its borders and under its control, leading to divisiveness and discord. Thus, the Holy City could not be designated until a king was chosen, since a strong central authority could avert these problems.[2]

The actual choosing of Jerusalem also involved its consecration, which, as mentioned earlier, required a king. Until Jerusalem was dedicated in this manner, it could not be considered to have been chosen, so the Torah speaks of its choosing as an event that would occur in the future. The location could not be revealed, since locating, occupying and dedicating the Holy City was a special function of the king, through which the royal line would be chosen for all time. Once David and Solomon had accomplished all this, they became worthy of fathering the royal line, and from then on, a king of Israel could be chosen only from their line.[3]

Actually, this place was chosen long before the time of David and Solomon, and it played a most important role in the lives of all the patriarchs, from Adam to Moses. For the above-mentioned reasons, as well as others of a deeper nature, this fact could not be stated explicitly in the Torah. Furthermore, as we shall see, there is evidence that the city was not actually called Jerusalem until after the death of Moses.

The earliest tradition regarding Jerusalem states that Adam was created from the same place where the Great Altar later stood in the Temple, "so that he should be created from the place of his atonement."[4] This is more than a mere legend; Maimonides states that the place of the Altar was later selected partially on the basis of this tradition.[5]

If Adam were created out of "dust from the ground," it was very special dust, that of the Altar. As discussed earlier, the concept of the Altar was to allow man to nullify his physical nature and rise above it. Thus, the very physical nature of man — the "dust from the ground" from which he was formed — was taken from the place that would allow him to overcome it and elevate it.

God then brought Adam to the Garden of Eden, but Adam sinned and was ejected. He returned to the place where he had been created, and, attempting to atone for his sin, built an altar on the Temple Mount and offered a sacrifice to God.[6] This altar remained as a permanent shrine where all people could worship God, until it was destroyed by the Flood in the time of Noah.[7] Adam remained in Jerusalem, immersing in a spring called Gichon as a further atonement for his sin.[8] There is evidence from tradition that Adam lived in Jerusalem all of his life.

When Cain and Abel brought their offerings to God, they did so on this altar built by Adam.[9] Abel had brought his best sheep, while Cain begrudgingly brought some wilted flax. For this reason, God accepted Abel's offering, but not that of Cain. Cain was so angry at being rejected that he eventually murdered his brother.

A view of Jerusalem and the Judean Hills, from the south, in a lithograph by David Roberts (c.1840).

A view of Mount Zion from the Mount of Olives.

Adam's altar in Jerusalem was destroyed by the Flood, but after the deluge, Noah returned there and rebuilt it.[10] Noah himself had been wounded in the Ark, so his son Shem offered the first sacrifices there.[11] As a result of this offering, God made his first covenant with mankind, that He would never again bring a flood that would destroy the world. The Altar in Jerusalem thus became the symbol of man's protection, guaranteeing that humanity would never again be destroyed by God.[12]

Shortly after this, Noah's youngest son Ham displayed gross disrespect toward his father, and Shem protected his father's honor. Noah then gave Shem a blessing, "May [God] dwell in the tents of Shem" (Genesis 9:27). This indicated that Shem's inheritance would include Jerusalem, which was where the Altar of God stood, and where the Temple would eventually be built.[13] Shem became the priest on this altar, bringing offerings and worshiping God. Thus, even at this early period, Jerusalem was an important place of worship; regarding this period the Psalmist said, "In Salem was set His tabernacle, and His dwelling place in Zion" (Psalms 76:3).[14]

Shem and his children occupied Jerusalem, and soon, together with his grandson Eber, Shem set up an academy where the word of God was taught.[15] Even at this early stage, Jerusalem had become a place of teaching, anticipating the important role that it would play after the establishment of the Sanhedrin.

When the city became large enough to require a government, Shem was crowned king and given the title of Malchi-tzedek.[16] This title actually means "king of Tzedek," *tzedek* meaning righteousness. Tzedek was a name frequently given to Jerusalem, because it was a place where righteousness was taught.[17]

Geographically, Jerusalem is divided into two parts, a "Lower City" to the east, and an "Upper City" on a higher elevation to the west.[18] These two parts are separated by a ridge running from north to south, which divides the city into these eastern and western sections. This division has existed since ancient times, with the boundary passing right through the area where the Temple would eventually be built.

The Lower City, which included the eastern slope of the Temple Mount, was known as Salem (Shalem) in ancient times. The Upper City, which included the western part of the Mount

and the place of the Altar, was known as the Land of Moriah.[19]

It was 340 years after the Flood that the Tower of Babel was built. Its builders were subsequently scattered over the face of the earth. The Canaanite tribes began to invade the Holy Land, and the Amorites occupied the western Upper City of Jerusalem, including the place of the Altar. As a sign of their disdain for Shem and his blessing, they destroyed the altar that he and Noah had built.[20] Shem and his people, however, retained control of Salem, the Lower City, and continued to maintain the academy there.

According to some legends, Abraham went to Jerusalem as a young child to study the traditions with Noah and Shem.[21]He might have learned then that a holy place existed, where Adam had been created and where the original Altar had been built, but he was not yet worthy of having the place revealed to him. As Abraham grew in his devotion to God, more and more he sought to ascertain the location of this most perfect place of worship. For many years he lived in Mesopotamia (presently Iraq), but when God told him to return to the Promised Land,

Opposite:
Top: *An entrance at the excavations at Nebi Samwil, tomb of the prophet Samuel.*
Bottom: *A newly restored promenade in the Old City. At the center are the remains of the famous Churvah Synagogue.*

Above: *Jerusalem abounds in contrasts: In the foreground are excavations of ancient civilizations. In the background is new construction that captures the mood of the Holy City's history.*

A 19th century lithograph of Sephardic Jews praying at the Kotel

Abraham directed his wanderings so that they brought him closer and closer to Jerusalem.[22]

Abraham soon became caught up in a war that was raging in the Holy Land, and his efforts were largely responsible for the outcome of this war. Although this war was fought on a physical plane, it was also symbolic of Abraham's battle against evil, and Abraham's victory thus had a twofold significance. After the decisive battle Shem came out to greet Abraham: "And Malchi-zedek, king of Salem, brought out bread and wine, and he was a priest to the highest God" (Genesis 14:18). He gave Abraham a blessing, declaring, "Blessed be Abram to God

According to many versions, this imposing medieval structure houses the tomb of King David

most high, maker of heaven and earth" (ibid. 14:19). In conferring this blessing, Shem was making Abraham the bearer of many of the traditions that had been handed down from the times of Adam and Noah.[23]

Shortly after this, God destroyed Sodom and Gemorrah, radically altering the balance of power in the Holy Land. One result was that eastern Jerusalem — Salem — the place of Shem's academy, increasingly began to come under the domination of the Philistines, who were occupying the area. In order to negotiate with them, Abraham went to the city of Gerar, where Abimelech, king of the Philistines, had his capital. Abraham had presented Sarah as his sister rather than his wife, and Abimelech had come close to adding her to his harem. After a serious epidemic and a disturbing dream, Abimelech finally gave Abraham free access to Jerusalem, saying, "Behold my land is before you, dwell wherever you please" (Genesis 20:15). The safety of Shem's academy was thus assured.

Abraham then finally had the son of his old age, Isaac. Abimelech realized that Jerusalem was important to Abraham, and now that he had an heir, there might eventually be a dispute regarding the city. Abimelech therefore approached Abraham and asked that he make a covenant, to which Abraham agreed. The two made a treaty that as long as a

"David" defender of the Holy City:
Below: *A monument to the Davidka, the nickname given to the crude, homemade mortar used by the Jews in the War of Independence*

Opposite: *Migdal David — a Herodian palace aptly named for the founder of Jewish Jerusalem, King David*

A touch of eternity: passing on a heritage of tradition and love to a grandson

descendant of Abimelech dwelt on the land, no descendant of Abraham would wage war against them. This covenant was later to be the reason why the Israelites could not capture the eastern part of Jerusalem.[24]

One tradition had not yet been given to Abraham, the location of the Altar. Before this could be revealed to him, Abraham had to be tested 10 times by God.[25] The 10th and most difficult of these tests occurred when God told Abraham to sacrifice his only beloved son, Isaac. God told Abraham, "Take your son, your only son, Isaac whom you love, and go to the land of Moriah, and bring him up for a sacrifice on one of the mountains that I will reveal to you" (Genesis 22:2). Even at this point, God did not tell Abraham the location of the holy Altar; it was not revealed to him until he had actually taken his son, embarked on the journey, and made all the preparations for the sacrifice. The only thing that Abraham knew was that he was going to Moriah, the western section of Jerusalem.

As Abraham and Isaac approached Jerusalem, they saw a ring of clouds over the Temple Mount, and they realized that this was the mountain where the Altar stood.[26] As they came closer, a pillar of fire pointed out the precise location of the Altar.[27] These clouds drove away the Amorites, and concealed

The Kotel, drenched with tears and ennobled by hope

The tiny, cramped Kotel area as it was before1967, when prayer demanded sacrifice and dedication

The cracks between the stones — then and now — were filled with handwritten supplications.

Abraham's activities on the mountain. Abraham rebuilt the Altar of Adam and Noah, and prepared to sacrifice Isaac on it, binding him as an offering. At the very last minute, God reprieved Isaac and substituted a ram for Abraham to sacrifice. With this, Abraham had the entire tradition, and he took Shem's place as the priest at the Altar on Mount Moriah.[28]

Abraham called the place of the Altar Yirah or Yiru (*Jeru*).[29] When this was united with the eastern part of the city, which was called Salem, the city got its present name, JeruSalem.[30] To this very day, the merit of Abraham and Isaac is concentrated there on the place of the Altar.[31]

Directly after this, Abraham purchased his first permanent plot in the Promised Land. Near Hebron, Abraham had discovered the cave of

Machpelah, where Adam and Eve were buried, and when Sarah died, he wished to bury her in this sacred cave. The land, however, belonged to Ephron the Hittite, who lived on a mountain just to the west of Jerusalem.[32] Ephron realized that Abraham's descendants would someday occupy the Holy Land; therefore, before he would sell Abraham the cave, he demanded that Abraham make an everlasting treaty that they would never take his city away by force. After the sale, Ephron made a huge monument, inscribed with the words of this treaty. As a result, the western part of Jerusalem was never taken by force, but was eventually purchased from Ephron's descendants.[33]

There appears to be a special providence involved in this, since this part of Jerusalem would contain the Great Altar. With regard to this Altar, the Torah states, "You shall not build it out of cut stones, for if you lift your sword against it, you have profaned it" (Exodus 20:22). The reason for this has been discussed earlier. However, if lifting a sword or iron tool against an inanimate stone can profane the Altar, how much more so can lifting a sword against a fellow human being! For this reason, of all places in the Holy Land, the place of the Altar was not taken by force, but was purchased.

Meanwhile, Isaac had not returned with Abraham, but

Prayer at the Kotel. Arching above the petitioners are the stones that were put in place over 2,000 years ago. Above the stones stood streets and houses.

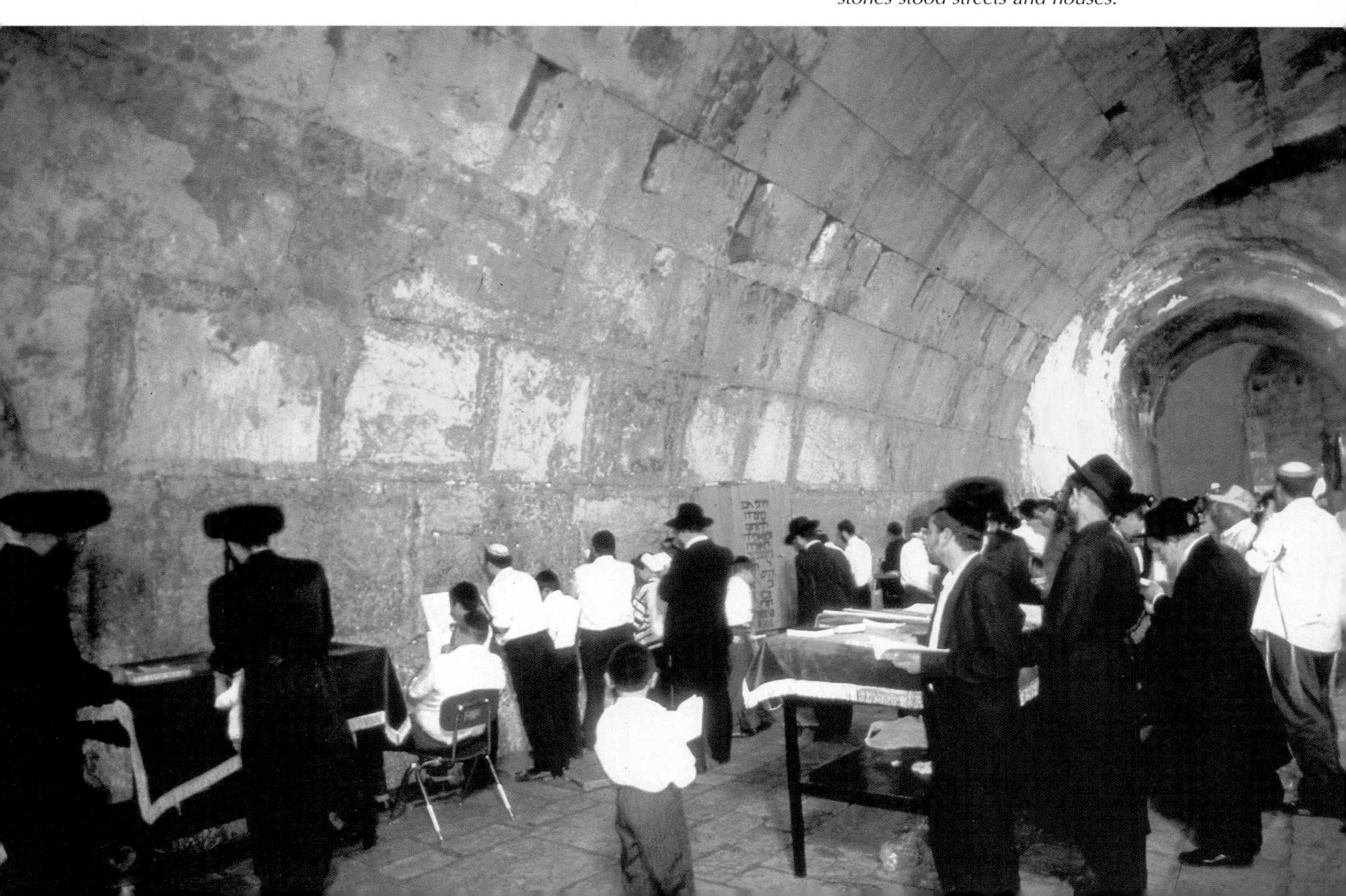

The Citadel at night. Once barren and abandoned, it is now a popular tourist attraction, bounded by a major thoroughfare.

Opposite: *The ancient fortress on Mount Zion*

remained in Jerusalem for three years while he studied in the Academy of Shem.[34] Isaac would frequently go to the place of the Altar to worship God, and there he ordained the daily afternoon service.[35] Although a number of tribes lived around Jerusalem at the time, the Temple Mount was uninhabited, since the people had been frightened away by the clouds and pillar of fire that had appeared on the mountain when Isaac was brought there for an offering.

While Isaac was in Jerusalem, Abraham sent his servant Eliezer to his cousins in the north to seek a wife for his son. Eliezer returned with Rebecca, and on this mountain she first met Isaac, who introduced her to the Academy of Shem in Jerusalem. Later, when it was discovered that Rebecca could not have children, Isaac returned to Jerusalem to the place of the Altar, and there he prayed for a child.[36]

Rebecca eventually conceived, but as her pregnancy progressed, she became disturbed by the unusual activity in her womb. Not knowing its meaning, she went to Jerusalem, where

The Cardo.
Originally built by the Romans and Byzantines, in the 12th and 13th centuries it functioned as a Crusader marketplace. It has been restored, beautifully and tastefully, as a major shopping mall in Jerusalem's Old City.

she prayed in the Academy of Shem, which was also a house of worship.[37] There she was informed that there were twins in her womb, and that Jacob, the younger son, would inherit the traditions from Abraham and Isaac. Isaac, however, was not aware of this, and he wished to give the tradition and blessing to Esau, the older son. It was because of Rebecca's knowledge that she connived to have the blessing given to Jacob instead of Esau.[38]

As a young boy, Jacob was drawn to Jerusalem, and he eventually became a student in Shem's academy. Shem's grandson, Eber, had set up a separate academy, and Jacob delved into his studies there as well.[39] Abraham died when Jacob was 15 years old, and at that time Jacob bought the birthright from Esau for a bowl of pottage.[40]

When Isaac grew old, the time came for him to give the blessing and the traditions to his children. He naturally wished to give the blessing and leadership to Esau, who was the older of the twins. Rebecca, however, knew the true nature of the two

Yoel Solomon Street, known for its boutiques, artists' shops and European-style cafés

boys, and she went so far as to disguise Jacob as Esau so that he would receive the blessing. When Jacob came in for the blessing, Isaac became aware of his identity, and also saw prophetically that Jacob's descendants were destined to build the Temple in Jerusalem.[41] Isaac then blessed him with the "dew of the heaven" (Genesis 27:28), alluding to the fact that he would be worthy of having revealed to him the place of the Holy of Holies, the door of all blessing.[42]

When Esau heard that Jacob had "stolen" his blessing, he was furious, and threatened to kill his brother. Jacob escaped to Jerusalem, to the Academy of Eber, where he remained for 14 years.[43] He then visited Beersheba, and prepared to go north to find a wife among his cousins there. On the way, he passed through Jerusalem, and coming to the Altar of Abraham in the evening, he prayed there, thus initiating the evening service.[44]

It is significant to note that Isaac had initiated the afternoon service in precisely the same place. The very fact that at least

two of the three daily prayers were initiated by the Patriarchs in Jerusalem clearly indicates that it is a focus of prayer. Indeed, this is yet another reason why all Jews face Jerusalem when they pray.

In the Holy of Holies, the Ark of the Covenant stood on a rock known as the *Evven Shetiyah*, the Foundation Stone. As discussed earlier, this spot was the "gate of heaven," the focus of prayer, and the place from which all prophecy emanated. Until this time, no man had known the location of this precise spot, even though the Patriarchs must have known that it was somewhere on the Temple Mount. Providence now guided Jacob so that he fell asleep precisely at this place.[45]

While sleeping on this rock, Jacob had his spectacular dream, where he saw the ladder standing on the ground, with its top reaching the heavens. This indicated that this place was the focus of spiritual elevation, through which a person could climb to the highest spiritual levels. When Jacob awoke from this prophetic dream, he realized the significance of the place and said, "How awesome is this place! It is none other than the house of God, it is the gate of heaven" (Genesis 28:17). On the place of the Ark, Jacob set up a stone as a monument and poured oil on it. Anticipating the Temple, he said, "This stone

that I have set up as a monument shall be God's house" (ibid. 28:22).

It was in this manner that the three most important features of the Temple were dedicated. The Chamber of the Sanhedrin was first dedicated by Shem, who built both an academy and a house of worship on this spot. The Altar was originally dedicated by Adam, and was rededicated by Abraham when he offered the ram in place of his son. Finally, the place of the Ark in the Holy of Holies was dedicated by Jacob, when he poured oil on the stone upon which he had slept.

Jacob then went to the north, to the land of Aram Naharayim, where he married his two cousins, Leah and Rachel. There he had 11 of his 12 sons, who would become the 12 Tribes of Israel. He then returned to the Holy Land.[46]

At this time, Jacob met with Esau for the first time since leaving home, and he and the 11 children who had been born bowed down to Esau.[47] Jacob then wrestled with the angel of

Opposite: *Meah Shearim street scenes.*
Top: *A primitive "shopping cart"*
Bottom: *Two modestly clad women on a stroll. The walls are community bulletin boards, plastered with layer upon layer of announcements.*

Above: *Yemin Moshe, which was founded in c.1860 by Sir Moses Montefiore. It was one of the first neighborhoods built outside the Old City walls. Today it is an exclusive upper class enclave.*

Homes in Machaneh Yehudah, a neighborhood that is best known for its teeming market

Opposite:
Top: *Nachalat Shivah, one of the first neighborhoods of the New City. Unlike many others, its construction was undertaken and financed by its own inhabitants.*
Bottom: *A street scene in the fervently Orthodox Geulah neighborhood*

Esau, who represented all the forces of evil, and when this angel could not overcome him, it was finally decided that Jacob would be the one to father the chosen people. The angel then gave him the name Israel (*Yisrael*), which means "a prince of God."[48]

Soon after this, God told Jacob to return to "the house of God," the place of the Holy of Holies in Jerusalem, where he had seen the vision of the ladder. Here God Himself confirmed what the angel had told Jacob, that he would father the chosen people and that his name would indeed be Israel. Jacob remained in Jerusalem for six months, worshiping and serving God in the place of the Holy of Holies.[49]

Right after this, Rachel gave birth to Jacob's 12th child, Benjamin. Providence had chosen Benjamin for a special task. It was in his portion of the Holy Land that the Altar and the Holy of Holies would be situated. There are several reasons for this. Benjamin was the only child born in the Holy Land, and he was the only one born after Jacob had been designated as Israel. Since he had not yet been born when Jacob's other children bowed down to Esau, he had never subjugated himself to Jacob's evil brother. Furthermore, as Jacob's youngest son, he

was closest to his father, learning all good traits from him.[50]

Eight years passed, and Joseph was 17 years old, while his oldest brothers were in their early 20s. At this time, an event occurred that would have a powerful influence on the Tribes of Israel, to a large extent designating their status for all times. This was the selling of Joseph by his brothers.

Of all the brothers, one had been particularly devoted to the study of the traditions that had been handed down from Abraham and the Academy of Shem. This was Judah; he had developed well, both in leadership and in a judicious nature. When the older brothers, Simon and Levi, wanted to kill Joseph, it was Judah who said, "What gain do we have if we slay our brother?" (Genesis 37:26). As a result of this, we find that Judah was already destined to be a leader among his brothers.[51] Benjamin, of course, remained innocent, since he was too young to take part in this episode.[52]

An old Yemenite neighborhood

In the very next account, the Torah speaks of the birth of Peretz to Judah and Tamar. As known from the genealogy, King David was a direct descendant of Peretz, and as we shall see, it was David who was destined to reveal Jerusalem as the city chosen by God.[53] This juxtaposition is deliberate, since it was due to Judah's role in saving Joseph that he became worthy to father the hereditary royal house of Israel.

It is known that Noah and his sons were given seven commandments by God. The first six of these forbid idolatry, adultery and incest, murder, robbery, cursing God, and eat-

The Russian Compound (built c. 1860). The large building is a courthouse. At the right is a jail.

ing flesh from a living animal. The seventh commandment requires the establishment of courts of law to uphold the first six.[54] Among other things, the Academy of Shem functioned as such a court of law, and we indeed find that when Esau threatened to murder Jacob, the latter replied that if he did, he would be judged by the judiciary of Shem.[55]

After the death of Shem and his grandson Eber, this judiciary was taken over by Isaac and Jacob. Of all the 12 sons of Jacob, we find none joining this judiciary other than Judah. Thus, when Tamar was suspected of adultery and so judged, we find that, as the youngest member of this judiciary, Judah was its spokesman. This is the common practice in capital cases.[56] Judah had thus proven himself in two fields, in leadership and in judgment.

From this point on, we find that Judah always took a leadership role among his brothers. When the brothers were to go back to Egypt for provisions, Judah took responsibility for the safety of Benjamin and convinced Jacob to let him go along with them. Later, when Joseph, who as viceroy of Egypt was

ארגון
תורה בעל פה
את נפשך. ד׳ ישמר צאתך ובואך מעתה ועד עולם
הללוי׳ הללו א-ל בקדשו הללוהו ברקיע עזו הללוהו
בגבורתיו הללוהו כרב גדלו, הללוהו בתקע שופר
הללוהו בנבל וכנור הללוהו בתף ומחול, הללוהו
במנים ועגב, הללוהו בצלצלי שמע הללוהו
בצלצלי תרועה, כל הנשמה תהלל יה הללוי׳ה.
תנא דבי רבי ישמעאל אלמלי
לא זכו ישראל אלא להקביל
פני אביהם שבשמים פעם אחת
בחדש דים אמר אביי הלכך צריך
למימרא מעמד מי זאת עולה מן
המדבר מתרפקת על דודה ויהי
רצון מלפניך ד׳ אלקי ואלקי אבותי
למלאות פגימת הלבנה ולא
בה שום מעוט ויהי אור הלבנה
החמה וכאור שבעת ימי
שהיתה קודם מעוטה שנאמר
המארות הגדולים ויתקים בנו
שכתוב ובקשו את ד׳ אלקיהם
דויד מלכם אמן:
למנצח בנגינות מזמור שיר. אלקים יחננו ויברכנו
אתנו סלה. לדעת בארץ דרכך בכל גוים ישועתך.
אלקים יודוך עמים כלם. ישמחו וירננו לאמים כי
מישר ולאמים בארץ תנחם סלה. יודוך עמים
עמים כלם. ארץ נתנה יבולה יברכנו אלקים
יברכנו אלקים וייראו אותו כל אפסי ארץ

Two faces of old Jerusalem:
Opposite: *The lone youngster personifies the charm and personality of Zichron Moshe. Is he waiting for a parent, playmate or study partner? Behind him is the modest building of one of Jerusalem's hundreds of small study centers. The huge poster contains the text of the monthly Sanctification of the Moon. It is printed in oversize letters, for the convenience of congregants crowding around it in the dim illumination of night time street lights.*

Above: *The bustling "main street" of Mea Shearim, lined by stores, papered with posters, peopled by shoppers, strollers and students. Shabbat is coming, and will not wait for the rain to stop.*

still not recognized by his brothers, wished to imprison Benjamin for stealing his cup, it was Judah who defended him. Finally, when Jacob was about to emigrate to Egypt to join Joseph, he sent Judah ahead to establish an academy so that the traditions would not be forgotten in Egypt.[57]

After Joseph revealed himself to his brothers, the Torah states that "he fell on Benjamin's neck and wept" (Genesis 45:14). According to tradition, at this moment Joseph saw the Altar and Holy of Holies built in Benjamin's portion, and he foresaw that they would eventually be destroyed.[58]

When Jacob blessed his sons, the destinies of these two tribes, Benjamin and Judah, were revealed. To Judah he said, "The scepter shall not depart from Judah, nor the staff of judgment from between his feet" (ibid 49:10). "The scepter" refers to the royal line, which would go to King David, a descendant of Judah, and remain in his family forever. "The staff of judgment

A vendor in the Bucharan market. The signs to the right of his stall say that the rabbinical court has separated the halachically prescribed tithes.

between his feet" indicates that the Hall of the Sanhedrin would be in the portion of Judah.[59] Judah was thus worthy of both leadership and judgment.

In Benjamin's blessing, Jacob said, "Benjamin is a tearing wolf, in the morning he devours his prey, and in the evening he divides the spoil" (ibid v.27). This alludes to the fact that the Great Altar would be in the portion of Benjamin, taking the sacrifices as its "prey," especially the daily offerings, morning and evening.[60] The Great Altar could therefore not be built in any other place than in the portion of Benjamin.[61]

The Promised Land would later be divided among the 12 Tribes by Joshua. The Temple Mount would be divided in half, so that the eastern part, where the Chamber of the Sanhedrin stood, would be in the portion of Judah, while the western half, with the Great Altar, would be in Benjamin's portion. This later helped locate the chosen city, because there was a firm tradition that the Altar would be in Benjamin's portion, and the Sanhedrin in that of Judah.[62]

It is significant to note the differences between these two brothers and their destinies. Judah was the fourth son of Leah, while Benjamin was the younger son of Rachel. While Judah was the symbol of leadership and judgment, Benjamin was the symbol of innocence and purity, never acting, but instead, allowing himself to be acted upon by God's providence. The royal line and the Sanhedrin were thus Judah's heritage, since these required boldness and leadership. The Altar, on the other hand, was in Benjamin's portion, since this is indicative of total submission to God — the Altar had to be built out of uncut stones, just as they had been created by God. Just as Judah protected Benjamin, so the royal house and the Sanhedrin would protect the sanctity of the Altar.

As time passed, Jacob and his sons died in Egypt. The last of the 12 brothers to die was Levi, who outlived Judah by seven years.[63] For these last seven years, Levi was the bearer and teacher of the traditions, and after he died, these were given to his grandson, Amram, who became the principal teacher

Robinson's Arch, from an 18th century color engraving.

In the Moslem Quarter of the Old City

Opposite: *The Arab souk (market) in the Old City, with wares displayed to attract passersby*

leader of the Israelites.[64] Very soon after Levi died the Israelites were enslaved, a condition that they would endure for over a century.

As leaders and bearers of the traditions, the tribe of Levi alone was able to avoid being enslaved. They had scrolls containing the traditions, and these they studied and taught to the other Jews. Alone of all the tribes, the Levites never worshiped idols in Egypt, and they also kept the covenant of circumcision.[65] It was thus no coincidence that Amram's two sons, Moses and Aaron, as well as his daughter Miriam, became the most important leaders of the Israelites in the generation of the Exodus.

The most spectacular event of the Exodus was the splitting of the Red Sea, and here again we find Judah and Benjamin in counterpoint. Before the sea could be split, the Israelites had to show an act of faith, demonstrating that they believed in the imminent miracle. Judah assumed the leadership role. The head of the tribe, Nachshon ben Aminadav, jumped into the Red Sea, anticipating that it would open; at the same time, the rest of the tribe attempted to repel the Egyptians with force. At the same time, the entire tribe of Benjamin entered the sea, submitting themselves totally to God's providence. It was at this time that Benjamin became worthy of having the Holy of Holies in his portion, in addition to the Altar, of which he was already worthy.[66]

In the desert, the Israelites frequently rebelled against God, questioning His providence over them — with the exception of the tribe of Levi. When the Israelites worshiped the Golden Calf, the only entire tribe which refrained from doing so was Levi. Thus, after the episode of the Golden Calf, the Torah tells us that "Moses said, 'Who is for God, to me!' and the sons of Levi gathered to him" (Exodus 32:26). Of all the tribes, only Levi kept the covenant of circumcision during the years in the

desert. While serving God was something new for many people in the other tribes, the Levites had never ceased doing so, even during the darkest days in Egypt. Thus, the Levites, and among them, the sons of Aaron as *Cohanim*-Priests were chosen to serve, first in the Tabernacle and later in the Temple.[67]

A 19th century scene in the Kidron Valley. At left is Yad Absalom, the tomb of King David's rebellious son.

The ultimate status of these special tribes is most evident in Moses' final blessing to all Israel. Since the man Judah had attained his status through his own efforts in the time of Jacob, Moses did not add anything significant in his blessing. In Levi's blessing, Moses gave the tribe permanent status as the guardians and officiants of the Temple: "They shall put incense before You, and a whole burnt offering on Your Altar" (Deuteronomy 33:10). Benjamin's blessing immediately follows that of Levi, indicating that the Altar on which the Levites and *Cohanim*-Priests would serve would be in Benjamin's portion.[68] Of Benjamin, Moses said, "Between his shoulders [God] shall dwell" (ibid. v.13). This indicates the final part of Benjamin's inheritance, indicating that the Holy of Holies would also be in his portion.[69]

When Moses sent spies to reconnoiter the Promised Land, one of the places that he wanted them to investigate apparently was Jerusalem. He thus told them, "Ascend to the mountain" (Numbers 13:17); and when the Torah speaks of a mountain in the Holy Land, it usually refers to Jerusalem. [70] We are later informed that "the Hittite, the Jebusite, and the Amorite dwell on the Mountain" (ibid. v.29), all these being closely related tribes. Regarding the Hittite, we already know that the family of

Ephron the Hittite had a settlement in the western part of Jerusalem, and from the fact that they are mentioned first, it appears that they were predominant. The Amorites are mentioned last, which might indicate that their influence had declined, at least at that time. The Jebusites were a very small Canaanite tribe, centered around Jerusalem. Even after the Jebusites left the area and were replaced by Philistines, the place was called Jebus, and its inhabitants, Jebusites. [71] The original Jebusites may have been among the tribes that left the Holy Land and settled in Africa before it was occupied by the Israelites.[72]

One of the main reasons why Moses wished to enter the Promised Land was to see Jerusalem, and possibly to build the Temple. He thus prayed to God, "O let me cross over, and let me see the good land across the Jordan, this good Mountain and the Lebanon" (Deuteronomy 3:25). According to tradition, the "good Mountain" refers to the Temple Mount in Jerusalem, while the "Lebanon" refers to the Temple itself. Jerusalem is the keystone of the Lebanon range, and the entire range derives its name from the fact that the Temple is built on one of its peaks. The Temple was called Lebanon,

An archeological section of David's Tower Museum. This dig has uncovered the center of the Citadel, one of the fortresses that protected Jerusalem.

A Crusader castle in the New City.

from the root *Laban* meaning white, since it "whitens the sins of Israel."[73]

Since Moses was not permitted to enter the Promised Land, God told him to reveal to Joshua the secret of where the chosen place would be. God told Moses, "Command Joshua and strengthen and fortify him, for he will cross over before these people, and bring them to inherit the land that you shall see" (Deuteronomy 3:28). Only Joshua knew this secret, and later, when David and Samuel wished to locate the chosen city, they had to consult the Book of Joshua.[74]

Dedication

An Old City alleyway

Moses did not live to enter the Promised Land; his disciple Joshua led the Israelites in the occupation. Even though Joshua knew that Jerusalem would be the chosen city, he did not reveal this to any of the tribes. This would have to wait until the permanent royal line was chosen, which did not occur until the time of David.

The first city in the Promised Land that the Israelites conquered was Jericho. Almost as soon as they entered the land, Joshua put aside the choicest fields near Jericho, later to be traded to the tribes in whose territory the chosen city would fall. This choice field was selected before the land was divided among the tribes; as territory common to them all, it was given over to the children of Moses' father-in-law Jethro for safekeeping.[1]

The Torah itself prescribes this as the method through which

An Old City excavation. This was the home of a Kohen during the second Temple Era.

Jerusalem should be chosen. In one place it states that the chosen place will be "from all your tribes" (Deuteronomy 12:5). Elsewhere, however, the Torah states that it will be "in one of your tribes" (ibid. v.14). The Torah is speaking of the place of sacrifice — the Altar — and initially, when the land was first divided, it would be in the portion of just one of the tribes, Benjamin. Then, however, it would be exchanged for the fields of Jericho, so that ultimately it would belong to all the tribes. Thus, when Jerusalem was eventually chosen and consecrated, it became the common property of all the tribes of Israel. As one place common to all, it had a strong effect in uniting the tribes.[2]

It is in the Book of Joshua that the first actual mention of Jerusalem occurs in the Bible. Here we see that Adoni-tzedek, king of Jerusalem, was involved in a battle with Joshua's forces and is defeated.[3] It is significant to note the resemblance of the name Adoni-tzedek to Malchi-tzedek, the title given to Shem when he became king of Jerusalem. This is because Jerusalem itself was called Tzedek — Righteousness — as discussed earlier, and Adoni-tzedek means "the lord of Tzedek." It was during the battle with Adoni-tzedek and his confederates that the Bible tells us the sun stood still for Joshua, aiding him in winning this battle.[4]

The Book of Joshua describes Adoni-tzedek as an Amorite king, so it appears that it was under the Amorites that the two parts of Jerusalem were united.[5] As discussed earlier, the western part of Jerusalem was called Jeru (*Yeru*), while the eastern part was known as Salem (*Shalem*). When the Amorite kings consolidated the two parts of the city, they also combined the names, calling the place Jerusalem.

From certain traditions, it appears that the Jebusites, who had made Jerusalem their capital, had left some 15 years before Joshua's conquest, and were replaced by the Philistine descendants of Abimelech.[6] The Philistines lived in Salem, the eastern district of Jerusalem, while the Hittite descendants of Ephron lived in the western half. By the time of Joshua's conquest, Jerusalem had already been united by the Amorite kings, and had been fortified and surrounded by a single wall.[7]After Joshua defeated the Amorites, it appears that Jerusalem again became divided into two districts.

The windmill, keystone of the Yemin Moshe neighborhood. It was built by Sir Moses Montefiore about 1860, to provide a livelihood for residents. It remains a cherished relic and a monument to Montefiore's generosity and the courage of Yemin Moshe's early pioneers.

Although Joshua defeated the king of Jerusalem, he did not

make any attempt to conquer the city itself.[8] This was because it was still protected by two covenants made by Abraham, one to Abimelech and the Philistines, and the other to Ephron and the Hittites. These ancient tribes were to have an important effect in giving Jerusalem special status.

Joshua then divided the land among the 12 tribes, according to a lottery and by the Urim and Thumim.[9] Looking at the border of Judah's portion, we see that it runs right through Jerusalem: "The border went up by the valley of Ben-Hinnom, to the shoulder of the Jebusite from the south — this is Jerusalem — and the boundary went up to the top of the mountain which overlooks the valley of Hinnom to the west"(Joshua 15:8). The mountain mentioned here is the Temple Mount, so we see that the boundary cuts right through the Temple area in Jerusalem. In describing the boundary of Benjamin, where the border runs from west to east, the Scripture states, "The boundary descended to the edge of the mountain that overlooks the valley of Ben Hinnom, to the shoulder of the Jebusite to the south" (ibid. 18:16).[10]

Opposite:
Top: *An ancient house on Beth-El Street*
Bottom: *The Shrine of the Book, home of the Dead Sea Scrolls and the Bar Kochba letters and artifacts, is a division of the Israel Museum. The building was designed in the shape of the covers of the pottery jars in which the Scrolls were stored.*

Above: *The Cardo. The five pillars supported the roof over the ancient marketplace. In the background are archways from the Roman and Byzantine period, one orginal and one reconstructed.*

For the most part, the portion of the tribe of Benjamin was north of that of Judah. In Jerusalem, however, the boundary took a sharp turn southward, cutting the Temple area in half, with the western side in Benjamin's portion, and the eastern side in that of Judah. When the Temple was later built, the Hall of the Sanhedrin was in the portion of Judah, while the Altar and Holy of Holies were in that of Benjamin.[11]

The eastern part of Jerusalem, occupied by the Philistines, thus fell into the portion of Judah. Because of Abraham's treaty with Abimelech and the Philistines, the tribe of Judah could not drive them out, and the Scripture thus states, "The sons of Judah could not drive out the Jebusites, the inhabitants of Jerusalem" (Joshua 15:63).[12] It was not until after the last descendants of Abimelech died after the time of Joshua that the tribe of Judah was able to conquer its portion of the city: "The children of Judah fought against Jerusalem and took it, smiting it with the sword and setting the city on fire"(Judges 1:8).

The western part of Jerusalem, which belonged to Benjamin,

Opposite:
Above: *Tombs of the prophets in the Kidron Valley, near the Valley of Hinnom. At the center is the tomb of the prophet Zechariah. The other structure contains the tombs of the priestly family of Hezir.*
Below: *Two of the most frequented graves on the Mount of Olives, places where one can almost always see people at prayer. They are the graves of Rabbi Chaim ben Attar (1696-1743), author of Or HaChaim* ***(Top)****; and Rabbi Chizkiyahu DiSilva (1659-1698), author of Pri Chadash.*

was inhabited by the Hittite descendants of Ephron, who had made a covenant with Abraham when the cave of Machpelah was purchased. Just as the sale of Machpelah had been permanent, so was this covenant, so the Benjaminites could not drive the Hittites out of their portion of Jerusalem. It is thus written, "The children of Benjamin did not drive out the Jebusites who inhabited Jerusalem" (ibid. v.21).[13] As mentioned earlier, whatever people lived in Jerusalem at the time were called Jebusites, whether they were Philistines or Hittites. Somewhat later, we still find that Jerusalem was not inhabited by Jews, since a Levite said of it, "We will not turn aside into a city of a foreigner, which is not of the children of Israel (ibid. 19:12).[14]

We thus see that of the original tribes who had lived in Jerusalem, the only ones who remained at the time of its conquest were the Hittite and the Amorite, the Philistines having arrived later. This is what the prophet Ezekiel meant when he said of Jerusalem, "Your father was an Amorite, and your mother was a Hittite" (Ezekiel 16:3,45).[15]

Excavation of a Kohen's house, from the Herodian Era. This room was a ritual bath.

No further mention of Jerusalem is found until after David's famous battle, where he defeated the Philistine warrior Goliath. Here the Scripture states, "David took the head of the Philistine and brought it to Jerusalem" (I Samuel 17:54). No reason is given; it is certain that David did not yet know that Jerusalem would be the chosen city. It appears, however, that the verse stresses that Goliath was "the Philistine" to teach that David brought his head to Jerusalem to indicate that Abraham's covenant with the Philistines was no longer in force, since the Philistines had been the ones to initiate the war against the Israelites. Although the treaty had been breached in the time of Judah's conquest of Jerusalem, and had been dishonored by the Philistines during their battles with Samson, the bringing of Goliath's head to Jerusalem was a concrete symbol that the covenant was no longer in force.[16]

Even though the place of the Temple ultimately had to be revealed prophetically, there was still an obligation for the one designated to found the royal line to attempt to find it logically.[17] All his life, David sought this most sacred place, and we thus find (Psalms 132:2-5):

Martef Hashoah, Chamber of the Martyrs, on Mount Zion, memorializes Jewish communities destroyed in the Holocaust.

Opposite:
The rusted wrecks of armored vehicles destroyed during the siege of Jerusalem in 1948. The hulks were left as monuments to the warriors who risked — and gave — their lives to save the city.

[David] swore to God,
made a vow to the Mighty One of Jacob:
I will not come in a tent as my house
I will not climb into my made-up bed
I will not allow my eyes to sleep
I will not let my eyelids rest
Until I find the place of God
the dwelling of the Mighty One of Jacob.[18]

David called God “the Mighty One of Jacob” in this psalm. This alludes to the fact that the place he sought was that of the Holy of Holies, which had been revealed to Jacob.[19]

Saul was still king over Israel at this time, and being jealous of David, he sought to kill him. David escaped to Ramah, where he stayed with the prophet Samuel. Earlier, Samuel had already anointed David as the future king, but there was still the requirement that the king find the place of the Altar. David and Samuel carefully went over all the traditions in order to ascertain logically the precise spot. Although Samuel was the greatest prophet of the time, he did not make use of his paranormal

The Citadel

Opposite:
Top: *Sunrise at the Kotel*
Bottom: *Tombstones on the Mount of Olives , opposite the Temple Mount*

powers, but guided David so that the latter would find the promised place.[20]

They knew the tradition that the Sanhedrin would have to be in the portion of Judah, near the Altar and Holy of Holies, which was to be in the portion of Benjamin.[21] It was therefore obvious that they would have to search along the border between Judah and Benjamin. They also knew that it would have to be the highest place on this border, since with regard to the Sanhedrin the Torah states, "You shall rise and go up to the place that the Lord your God shall choose" (Deuteronomy 17:8). Samuel also

knew that the secret of the chosen place had been revealed to Joshua, so they carefully looked at the description of the border between Judah and Benjamin as described in the Book of Joshua. Here they saw that the border "went upward" as far as the "mountain overlooking the valley of Ben-Hinnom" (Joshua 15:8), which was the highest place on the border. It was thus ascertained that the mountain upon which the Temple would be built was in Jerusalem, and all that was needed now was to determine the precise place of the Altar.

Saul was later killed in battle, and at the age of 30, David was crowned king of his tribe Judah in Hebron. There he remained for seven years until the time became ripe for him to take Jerusalem. There was a tradition that the one who would conquer the chosen city would inherit the royal house of Israel for all time. David had already determined the place, and before he went forth to Jerusalem, he was anointed by all Israel as king.[22]

By force, David occupied the eastern half of Jerusalem, where the Philistines originally lived, and which had earlier been captured and destroyed by the tribe of Judah. Since the place of the Altar could not be tainted by blood, he did not attack the western half in the portion of Benjamin, but he did remove the monuments containing Abraham's treaty, which had been erected by the Hittite sons of Ephron.[23] This was enough to indicate that David was in control of the city and thus had established himself in the hereditary role of king. David also reunited the two parts of the city and built a wall around it.[24]

There was no state of war between David and the Hittites; we later find that the Israelites dwelt together with them in peace.[25] David's conquest of the Philistine portion of Jerusalem, however, was seen as an act of war, and soon after this we find that they began to wage war against David in the Valley of Raphaim, which was to the south of Jerusalem.[26]

After all these wars, David finally brought the Ark of God to Jerusalem, knowing that it was the chosen city. He set aside a special place for the Ark, as we find, "They brought the Ark of God and set it in its place, in the midst of the tent that David had made for it" (II Samuel 6:17).[27] A place for the Altar had not yet been determined, however, and they still sacrificed in Gibeon, outside of Jerusalem.[28] Whenever David acquired gold or other precious things in his conquests, he brought them to Jerusalem to be dedicated to the House of God that would be built there.[29]

An "embrasure" in the wall of Jerusalem. The narrow opening was used by archers and, in later years, by riflemen.

Opposite: *Excavations at the Citadel*

The commandment to build the Temple became an obligation as soon as peace was attained by the king. Such peace was achieved in the time of David.[30] David very much wanted to build the House of God, and the Scripture states, "When the king dwelt in his palace and God gave him rest from all his enemies round about, the king said to Nathan the prophet,'See now, I live in a house of cedar, but God's Ark dwells in a curtain tent' " (ibid. 7:2).[31] David was informed that he could not be the one to build the Temple since his hands were sullied with blood, as he later told his son Solomon, "God's word came to me saying, `You have shed much blood and have made great wars, you shall not build a house to My Name, because you have shed much blood in My sight' " (I Chronicles 22:8). If even lifting iron against a stone renders it unfit for the Altar, how much more so was a king who had shed human blood unfit to build the Temple of God.[32] Still, because David had been the one to occupy the chosen city, he was the one to earn the hereditary royal house of Israel for all time, as God told him through the prophet Nathan, "Your throne shall be established forever" (II Samuel 7:16).

A row of houses adjoining the Churva Synagogue in the Jewish Quarter. One of them was the residence of Rabbi Shmuel Salant, who for 70 years in the 19th and early 20th centuries was a member of the rabbinate and Chief Rabbi of the Holy City.

The final step was the revelation of the place of the Altar, and the Bible describes this most graphically.[33] God became angry at David and tempted him to count the Israelites, bringing on them a terrible plague. David then prayed to God for forgiveness. He saw an angel standing on the threshing floor of Arnon the Jebusite. The prophet Gad then told David, "Go raise an altar to God on the threshing floor of Arnon the Jebusite" (II Samuel 24:18), and David did so, bringing offerings to God as an atonement.

The place of the Altar was thus revealed to David. This was the same place where Adam was created, and where he had offered the first sacrifice. There Cain and Abel as well as Noah had brought offerings to God. On that very spot Abraham had bound his son Isaac when he was so commanded by God.[34] When this was revealed to David, he said, "This is the house of the Lord, God, and this is the Altar of sacrifice for Israel" (I Chronicles 22:1).

One thing that still must be clarified is the reason for the manner in which the place of the Altar was revealed. Why did it have to be revealed through a sin, and only after David's subsequent repentance? Furthermore, the Scripture states that "God became angry at Israel" (II Samuel 24:1), but does not give any reason for it.

If one looks at the verse immediately before this, however, one will find a mention of Uriah the Hittite, one of David's generals. The Midrash states that God became angry at David and Israel because David had caused the death of Uriah.[35] This Uriah was the husband of Bathsheba, and when David wished to take Bathsheba for a wife, he sent Uriah to the front where he was killed. The fact that David had sent a man to certain death in order to marry his wife was considered a great wrong, and David was severely rebuked by the prophet Nathan.[36]

The Talmud teaches that King David never actually became involved with Bathsheba out of lust, since he had long since perfected himself spiritually. The only reason for this entire episode was to teach the ways of repentance, since it is clearly evident that God eventually forgave David.[37] The lesson is that

Top:
Beautifying a Meah Shearim dwelling

Bottom:
An alleyway in Meah Shearim

The "Upper Fountain of Siloam" in the Valley of Jehosaphat, the main water source of ancient Jerusalem.

Opposite: *The ornate doors of the famous Beth-El synagogue in the Old City*

no matter how great a sin a person commits, if he is truly contrite in asking God to forgive him, the sin is wiped away. Nothing can stand before repentance.[38]

The main idea of the Altar was that of forgiveness and atonement. Therefore, the episode involving Bathsheba, which was meant to teach the ways of repentance, was ultimately also the means through which the location of the Altar was revealed.[39] It was almost as if the power of repentance revealed by David would be built into the Altar. In a similar vein, it should be noted that it was the son born to David and Bathsheba — Solomon — who eventually built the Temple.

But it is also important to note exactly how God brought this about. As a result of David's misdeed with Bathsheba and her husband Uriah, God enticed him to take a census of the Israelites. God caused David to forget the injunction, "When you take the sum of the children of Israel, according to their

ישיבת המקובלים קהל קדוש חסידים
בית אל
ותחזינה עינינו בשובך לציון ברחמים

number, then each man shall give a ransom for his soul to God when you number them, that there be no plague among them when you number them" (Exodus 30:12).[40] The atonement in the time of Moses consisted of a half-shekel given toward the building of the Tabernacle. The census was taken by counting the total number of half-shekels, and Moses used this silver to build the foundations of the Tabernacle.[41] As a result, every Israelite had a part in the foundation of the Tabernacle. Furthermore, it is evident that the idea of properly counting the Israelites was very closely related to the building of the Tabernacle and the Temple.

Thus, when God was ready to reveal the place of the Altar, he did so by tempting David to commit a wrong very closely related to the sanctuary, namely, counting the Israelites without the atonements of the half-shekel. The sin itself thus was bound to the very foundation of the Temple. When David subsequently repented and was forgiven, his repentance also became a part of the Altar's foundation.

David had thus done everything necessary to find the Altar according to Torah law. First, he had sought it himself. Finally he had been worthy of having the place revealed to him by Gad the prophet.[42] David then bought the place of the Altar from Arnon the Jebusite for 50 silver shekels. He also collected 50 shekels from each of the 12 tribes of Israel, buying the entire city of Jerusalem from Arnon for 600 gold shekels. The entire city of Jerusalem thus became the common property of all Israel.[43]

Although David could not build the Temple himself, he prepared for its construction, assembling all the necessary materials.[44] David dug the foundations of the Temple, particularly in the place of the Altar.[45] He also gave Solomon a complete written plan of how the Temple should be built, as he had received the tradition from the prophet Samuel and from Ahitofel.[46] David

gave the pattern to Solomon, saying, "All is in writing, as God has given me wisdom by His hand on me, all the works of this plan" (I Chronicles 28:19).[47]

Before David died, he made sure that his son Solomon was anointed as king. This was done on the spring of Gichon in Jerusalem.[48] Solomon took his father's place as king over all Israel, and one of his first acts was to complete the wall of the Holy City.[49] But Solomon's greatest accomplishment was building the Temple of God, in the exact spot that had been designated by God from the beginning of creation.[50]

The Bible thus says, "Then Solomon built the house of God in Jerusalem, on Mount Moriah, where there had been a vision to his father, which he prepared in the place of David on the threshing floor of Arnon the Jebusite"(II Chronicles 3:1). Mount Moriah, of course, was the place where Abraham had bound his son Isaac as a sacrifice, and this was the place revealed to David to be the Altar of God.[51]

Opposite:
*Exterior **(Top)** and interior **(Bottom)** of The Churva synagogue*

Above: *The Churva's arch.*
The synagogue was known as The Churva (Ruin), because it was built on the ruins of the study hall of Rabbi Yehudah Chassid, who led his disciples to Jerusalem in the late 17th century. It was the Old City's largest synagogue until the Jordanians destroyed it during their occupation, from 1948-1967.

Opposite: *The small Kotel area in c.1946.*

Above: *Two young shoppers on Meah Shearim Street.*

The Temple built by Solomon stood for 410 years, and during this time, Jerusalem was the spiritual center for all Israel. Finally, due to the many sins of the people, God allowed both Jerusalem and the Temple to be destroyed by the Babylonians, led by King Nebuchadnezzar. After a 70-year exile, the Temple was rebuilt under the leadership of Ezra and Nehemiah, with the exact place of the Altar once again revealed by one of the last remaining prophets.[52] This second Temple stood for 420 years, and Jerusalem was once again a center of worship and Torah for the entire Jewish people.[53]

Jerusalem and the second Temple were finally destroyed by the Romans in the year 70 C. E.

On the same day of the year both the first and second Temples were destroyed, and Jerusalem was laid waste. This was the ninth day of the Hebrew month of Ab, better known as Tisha b'Av.[54] This day has been one of national mourning and fasting ever since.

Even though the Temple has been destroyed, the area upon

In the Moslem Quarter

which it stood still retains its special sanctity. Today, since the modes of ritual cleansing no longer exist and we are therefore all ritually unclean, it is forbidden to enter the area of the Temple Mount.[55] The Western Wall of the Temple Mount — the *Kotel* — is still a shrine to Jews all over the world.

There are many things that the Jew does to recall the destruction of Jerusalem. It is a custom in some circles to leave a small square of one's house unplastered to commemorate this tragedy.[56] As mentioned earlier, this is the reason why the groom breaks a glass at the wedding ceremony. One who sees Jerusalem in its state of destruction must rend his clothing, just as one who is in mourning.[57]

Our sages teach us that there is no joy before God since the time that Jerusalem and the Temple were destroyed.[58] Whoever mourns for Jerusalem will be worthy to witness its redemption.[59]

Rebirth

An Old City alleyway

When a Jew says, "Next year in Jerusalem," it is more than just a prayer that he may visit the Holy City, or even that he should settle there. It is a prayer for the entire future of the Jewish people, and for the world in general. So closely is Jerusalem tied with the ultimate future and coming of the Messiah that saying "Next year in Jerusalem" is nothing less than a prayer for the inception of the Messianic Age.

The belief in the coming of the Messiah led the Jew to be optimistic about the future. Even in the darkest exile, under the worst persecutions, the Jew knew that he would survive, and that if not he, his descendants would be worthy of seeing the Messiah, when both the Jew and the world in general would be brought to a state of perfection. The Messiah would eventually bring the Jew out of his long exile, end the persecutions, and bring him back to the Holy Land where he could live in peace

An old Yemenite neighborhood

Opposite: *A large Jerusalem home from the period of the Mishnah, reputed to be that of Kalba Savua, father-in-law of Rabbi Akiva. He was one of the three very wealthy men who sustained Jerusalem during the Roman siege that ended in the destruction of the Second Temple.*

and pursue the Torah to its fullest extent.

This does not mean that the Messiah will necessarily be a superhuman being, or even a superman. He will be an outstanding saint, with extraordinary leadership abilities, and will be able to bring about the redemption of Israel without suspending any laws of nature. Of course, if the Jews are worthy, this redemption can come through miracles, but if not, it will still come, but without miracles in an orderly series of events. [1]

It was this messianic optimism that led to the rise of Zionism, as a movement of national liberation — the first such movement in the world. The Jew knew that things would eventually have to improve and that the redemption would have to come — God Himself had promised this — and if it did not come through miracles, it would have to come about through human effort. Maybe some did not realize it, but the people who led the rebirth of the Holy Land were taking part in the first stages of the Messianic drama, which includes the building of the land. As the time of the redemption drew near, God sent a spirit of enthusiasm to the Jewish people, impelling them to return and recultivate the Land of Israel.

Thus, there is a tradition that the Land of Israel would have a measure of political freedom before the coming of the Messiah.[2] According to some, this will occur with the permission of the other nations.[3] There is also a tradition that the land will be cultivated before the Messiah reveals himself, based on the prophecy, "O mountains of Israel, let your branches sprout forth, and let you yield your fruit to My people of Israel, for their time has almost come" (Ezekiel 36:8).[4]

As the most holy place in the Land of Israel, Jerusalem is the most important city that must be rebuilt there.[5] There is a tradition that the ingathering of the exile and the rebuilding of

Opposite: Painting of a Jerusalem street scene

Above: A father and his two young sons at the Kotel

Jerusalem will go hand in hand, as the two most important preludes to the coming of the Messiah. According to this tradition, first a small percentage of the exile will return to the Holy Land, and then Jerusalem will come under Jewish control and be rebuilt. Only then will the majority of Jews in the world return to their homeland. It is thus written, "God is rebuilding Jerusalem, He will gather the dispersed of Israel" (Psalms147:2).[6]

There are many other prophecies that link the ingathering of the exile with Jerusalem. Thus, the redemption of Jerusalem and its return to Jewish hands is seen as the first definite sign of the redemption. As the prophet Isaiah said, "Break forth in joy, sing together, O you ruins of Jerusalem, for God has comforted His people, He has redeemed Jerusalem" (Isaiah 52:9). The prophet Zechariah sees the return to Jerusalem as the beginning of the total renaissance of the Jewish people: "I will bring them, and they will dwell in the midst of Jerusalem; and they will be My people, and I will be their God in truth and in righteousness" (Zechariah 8:8). Thus, the relationship between the regaining of the original (old) city of Jerusalem and the fact

הכנסת אורחים הגדול תפארת ציון וירושלם
נוסד על ידי שמואל לעוי בעזרת-ע"י נדיבי אמריקה
JMMIGRANTS SHELTER TIFERET ZION V. JERUSALEM
FOUNDED BY SAMUEL LEVY BY THE SUPPORT OF AMERICAN JEWISH FINLANTHROPISTS

Opposite: The famous sundial clock — built a century ago and still in use. At the upper right is a standard electric clock; at the upper left is a clock which records time according to the Arab system.

Above: The Menorah at the Knesset. A gift from the British Parliament to the State of Israel, it was designed by Benno Elkan. The engravings depict scenes from Jewish history.

that many thousands of young people are now finding their way back to Judaism is more than mere coincidence.

There is also another important reason why the ingathering of the exile must precede the coming of the Messiah. There is a tradition that before the Messiah comes, the concept of prophecy will once again flourish among the Jewish people.[7] Furthermore, according to the final words ever spoken by a prophet, Elijah will return as a prophet and announce the coming of the Messiah: "Behold I will send you Elijah the prophet before the coming of the great and terrible day of God" (Malachi 3:23). [8] This is necessary because the Messiah will be a king, and a king can be anointed only by a prophet. [9] Besides this, the Messiah himself will be a prophet, the greatest of them all, second only to Moses. [10]

Thus, the re-establishment of the concept of prophecy is very important in the unfolding of the Messianic drama. This, however, requires a number of conditions. First of all, prophecy can usually take place only in the Land of Israel, and not in any other land. [11] The Land of Israel, however, is not conducive to prophecy at all times. Before prophecy can exist in

of Israel, it must be inhabited by the majority of Jews in the world.[12]

This is actually evident in the Torah's words regarding prophecy. The Torah states that, "The Lord your God will raise up a prophet from your midst" (Deuteronomy 18:15); and from this verse the sages derive the teaching that prophecy can only exist in the Holy Land.[13] However, the Land of Israel is only called "your midst" when it is populated by all, or at least the majority, of the Jewish people. It is through the concentrated spiritual energy of the entire Jewish people that prophecy exists, and such concentration is only effective in the Land of Israel.[14]

One of the most important events in the Messianic era will be the rebuilding of the Holy Temple. Indeed, according to Rambam (*Maimonides*), it is the act of building the Temple that will establish the identity of the Messiah beyond all shadow of a doubt.[15] There are, however, many things involving the Temple that can only be ascertained prophetically, such as, for example, the precise location of the Altar.

When Ezra rebuilt the Temple after the Babylonian exile, the place of the Altar had to be revealed prophetically, and the same will apparently be true when the Temple is rebuilt in the Messianic Age.

Rambam (*Maimonides*) states that the Sanhedrin will also be re-established before the coming of the Messiah.[16] There are a number of arguments for this. Firstly, the Messiah will be preceded by a prophet, who will be identified as Elijah. As discussed earlier, however, a prophet can only be accredited by the Sanhedrin. This is logical, since the message of a prophet affects all Israel; and unless there was a formal means of accreditation, any person could claim to be a prophet, whether he truly had this gift or not. Indeed, there is a tradition that Elijah will initially appear before the great Sanhedrin in Jerusalem in order to be recognized by this body.[17]

Another argument for this is that the Messiah will be a king over Israel, and a king can only be crowned by the Sanhedrin. Thus, before the Messiah can be recognized as king, there must be a Sanhedrin in existence. Establishing a Sanhedrin would require total agreement on the part of every religious leader in the Holy Land, and such agreement itself would help make us worthy of the Messiah.

Opposite:
Top: *A bunker and trenches at Ammunition Hill, a Jordanian stronghold captured during the Six-Day War*
Bottom: *The remains of pillars in the Cardo*

A fortress turret in the Old City

A typical courtyard and building in the Old City

Opposite: *The tomb of the prophet Zechariah*

According to the prophecies, the Messiah will begin his career in Jerusalem. The prophet Zechariah thus said, "Rejoice greatly, O daughter of Zion, sound the trumpet, O daughter of Jerusalem, behold your king is coming, he is righteous and triumphant — a poor man riding on a donkey" (Zechariah 9:9).[18] One reason he might come to Jerusalem first is to be recognized by the Sanhedrin.

There are prophecies that there will be a "War of Gog and Magog" around Jerusalem. [19] According to this tradition, when the nations hear of the successes of the Jews, they will gather to do battle against them near Jerusalem, led by "Gog, the king of Magog." This battle will symbolize the final war between good and evil, where in Jerusalem all evil will ultimately be vanquished. [20]

According to tradition, there will be two Messiahs, the "Messiah son of David," of the Davidic line, and the "Messiah

The Moslem Quarter

Opposite: *Newly built apartments in the Old City*

son of Joseph," from the tribe of Ephraim. These again represent Jacob's two wives — David from Judah and Leah, and Joseph from Rachel. The Messiah son of Joseph will be the one who will lead the Israelites to victory in the war of Gog and Magog; he will die in battle. Since the Messiah son of David will be the one to rebuild the Temple, like Solomon, his hands must be unsullied by war and bloodshed. [21]

The main idea of the Messiah includes two concepts. First, the Messiah will redeem and perfect the Jewish people, creating of them a perfect society and bringing them back to an optimal spiritual status. All Jews will return to the teachings of the Torah and rise to a very high spiritual level, which will even include universal prophecy. On this level, the Jews will be able, in turn, to perfect the world around them, teaching all nations how to live in peace under the law of God. The society of mankind will thus be rectified and perfected for all time.

All this will be centered in Jerusalem. The main purpose of the ingathering of the exile will be to worship God in Jerusalem, as the prophet Isaiah foretold, "It will be on that day, that a great Shofar will be sounded, and those lost in the land of Assyria will come, and those dispersed in the land of Egypt, and they will worship God on the holy mountain in Jerusalem" (Isaiah 27:13). There is a tradition that the *Shofar* (ram's horn) that will be sounded to gather the exile will be from the ram that was offered by Abraham in place of Isaac. This took place on the Great Altar in Jerusalem, and it is there that the people will be assembled. [22]

Then Jerusalem will become the great center of worship and instruction for all mankind. God thus told His prophet, "I will return to Zion, and I will dwell in the midst of Jerusalem, and Jerusalem will be called the City of Truth and the Mountain of the Lord of Hosts, the Holy Mountain" (Zechariah 8:3). This will begin the period when the teachings of God will be supreme over all mankind: "For the Lord of Hosts will be king in Mount Zion and in Jerusalem, and before His elders there will be glory" (Isaiah 24:23).

All peoples will then come to Jerusalem to seek God. The prophet Zechariah describes this graphically: "Many people and mighty nations will come and seek the Lord of Hosts in Jerusalem.... In those days, ten men out of all the nations shall take hold of the corner of the garment of every Jew and say, 'We will go with you, for we have heard that God is with you' " (Zechariah 8:22,23). In Jerusalem, the Jewish people will thus become established as the spiritual and moral teachers of all mankind.

OUTSIDE CITY

At that time, Jerusalem will become the spiritual capital of all mankind.[23] This is dramatically described in the prophecy of Isaiah (Isaiah 2:2-4):

And it shall come to pass in the end of days
that the Mountain of God's house
shall be set over all other mountains
and lifted high above the hills
and all the nations shall come streaming to it.
And many peoples shall come and say:
Come, let us go up to the Mountain of God
to the house of the God of Jacob
and He will teach us His ways
and we will walk in His paths.
For out of Zion shall go forth the Torah
and God's word from Jerusalem.
And He will judge between nations
and decide between peoples.
And they will beat their swords into plowshares
and their spears into pruning hooks,
Nation shall not lift up sword against nation
neither will they practice war any more.

Yemin Moshe, an old neighborhood that has become an upscale, bucolic enclave in the New City

Eye of the Universe

One of the Old City's many arched entrances; a step into eternity

The last question we must discuss is why God chose the Land of Israel as the chosen land; and in particular, why He chose Jerusalem as its spiritual focus. Of course, we have seen how the Altar in Jerusalem played an important role from the time of Adam, but still, why was it this spot in particular that was chosen, and none other?

If you look at a map, you will see that the geographical location of the Land of Israel virtually guaranteed that it would play a key role in the tides of civilization. The Old World consisted of two great land masses, Eurasia (Europe and Asia) and Africa. It was impossible to travel from Eurasia to Africa without passing through the Holy Land. Therefore, every conqueror, every civilization that passed from one continent to the other, had to pass through the Holy Land and come in contact with the Jew. The Land of Israel thus interacted with virtually every great civilization, and all of them

were, to some degree, influenced by the teachings of the Torah.

Besides being a gateway between north and south, the Holy Land is part of the keystone link between east and west. There are mountains in Israel where a cup of water spilled on the western slope will eventually flow into the Atlantic Ocean, while one spilled on the eastern slope will flow into the Pacific. Today, these oceans are linked by the Suez Canal, but in the past, most caravan routes linking the Atlantic and Pacific passed directly through the Holy Land.

The Land of Israel was therefore literally the crossroads of civilization. Its capital and spiritual center, Jerusalem, was the focus of a process where the Jew would interact with all peoples,

Opposite: *The famous Ben Yehudah Pedestrian Mall. Sabras and tourists, families and anyone looking for a break from Jerusalem's hectic traffic or life's demanding dilemmas come to this oasis to stroll, shop or dine in the heart of the city.*

Above: *The past and the present: The Shrine of the Book — repository of the Dead Sea Scrolls — as the foreground to the Knesset — seat of the Israeli parliament.*

Opposite: A typical Old City building, with a broad courtyard and flanked by a narrow public alley

Above: Rothschild Gardens in the Old City

absorbing all the wisdom of the ancient world, while at the same time touching every great civilization with the wisdom of the Torah. It was thus taught that "Jerusalem is the center of the world."[1] God also told His prophet, "This is Jerusalem, I have set her in the midst of nations, and countries are around her" (Ezekiel 5:5). Considering both the centrality of its location and its spiritual influence, it is not at all surprising that Jerusalem today is a sacred city to the majority of the world's population.

Even today, when land routes are no longer as important as they were in the past, Jerusalem is still a center of human concern. One need only to think of how Providence placed the major portion of the world's supply of oil — the main source of transportation energy — within a stone's throw of Jerusalem. The world would otherwise not give the Holy City a second thought, except perhaps as an ancient sacred shrine. As it is, decisions made in Jerusalem today can influence even the greatest world powers. Jerusalem thus still occupies an important role in the councils of nations. All this is certainly more than mere coincidence.

A Mea Shearim wall, serving as a public bulletin board, with layer upon layer of announcements — Jerusalem's equivalent of the town crier

Opposite: *The "Little Kotel." Found in the Moslem Quarter, it is an extension of the Wall, with buildings leaning against it.*

On a much deeper level, however, we see Jerusalem not only as a center of civilization, but also as the very center of creation.

As discussed earlier, the most important single object in Jerusalem was the Ark, containing the Tablets and the Original Torah. This stood in the Holy of Holies on an outcrop of bedrock known as the *Evven Shetiyah*, literally, the Foundation Stone.[2] The Talmud states that it is called the "Foundation Stone" because it was the foundation of the universe. As the Talmud explains, this is because it was the very first point at which God began the act of creation.[3]

This is based on the teaching that creation began at a single point, and from this point, the universe unfolded until God decreed that it should stop. This is the significance of Shadai, which is one of God's Names. It comes from the word *Dai*, meaning "enough," and it indicates the Attribute through which God stopped the expansion of creation at a certain stage.[4]

Here we must seek to understand why creation had to begin at a single point, and what is the significance of this point. Why could creation not have been brought into existence all at

Shoneh Halachot Street, in the beautifully and tastefully rebuilt Jewish Quarter of the Old City

Opposite: *A statue at Yad Vashem. Its depiction of the grieving nation needs no plaque or explanation.*

once? Why did it all have to emanate from a single point in space?

The answer to these questions involves an understanding of the entire concept of the spiritual and physical, as well as the difference between the two. There are numerous discussions regarding the difference between the physical and the spiritual, but this difference is often not spelled out precisely. Very closely related is the question of why God created a physical world in the first place. God Himself is certainly spiritual, as is the ultimate purpose of creation. It is therefore somewhat difficult to understand the need for a physical world at all.

With a little insight, the difference between the spiritual and the physical is readily apparent. In the physical realm, there is a concept of physical space, while in the spiritual this concept is totally absent. All that exists in the spiritual realm is conceptual space. Two things that are similar are said to be close, while things that are different are said to be far from one another. While in the physical world it is possible to push two different things together, this is impossible in the spiritual realm.[5]

We see a good example of this in the case of the teachings

The sign at the top, in three languages, alerts the poor to one of the Hareidi community's many services for the needy

involving angels. It is taught that one angel cannot have two missions, while two angels cannot share the same mission.[6] There is no spatial concept unifying an angel. Therefore, if an angel had two missions, by definition it would become two angels. On the other hand, if two angels had the same mission, there could be no physical space separating them, and by definition they would be a single angel.[7]

We now begin to see why a physical world is needed. If only a spiritual world existed, there would be no way in which two different things could be brought together. Because they are different, by definition they are separated, and there would be no physical space in which they could be "pushed" together.

Spiritual entities, however, can be bound to physical objects, very much as the soul is bound to the body. The only way, then, in which two different spiritual entities or forces can be brought together is when they are bound to the same physical thing, or to two physical things which themselves are brought together.

A good example of this involves the impulses for good and evil in man, respectively known as the *Yetzer Tov* and the *Yetzer HaRa*. In a purely spiritual sense, good and evil are opposites, which can never be brought together. Without man's physical body, they could not be brought together in a single entity; indeed, in angels, which are purely spiritual, good and evil cannot co-exist.[8] It is only in a physical body that good and evil can be brought together, and man therefore had to be created

A section of the chomah, the protective medieval wall around the Holy City. The openings at the top are for archers and riflemen.

with such a body before he could have within himself the combination of good and evil that would allow him to have free will and free choice.[9]

God created many different spiritual concepts, forces and entities with which to create and direct the universe. Spiritual concepts can consist of such opposites as good and evil, or justice and mercy, as well as the basic concepts of giving and receiving, which are the spiritual roots of masculinity and femininity. There are also countless angels and spiritual potentials, all interacting to bring about the processes through which the universe is directed and guided.

All these are different, and in some cases opposite, and there would be no way for them to come together so that they could act in concert. The only way in which all spiritual forces can be brought together is for all of them to be associated with a single physical point. This point is the *Evven Shetiyah* — the Foundation Stone of all creation.

Jerusalem's original name was Shalem (Salem), coming from the same root as *Shalom*, meaning peace. One of the main concepts of Jerusalem is peace, as it is written, "Seek Jerusalem's peace" (Psalms 122:6). But, as the *Zohar* explains, this peace is not only in the physical world; it also implies peace in the spiritual world.[10] The meaning of this is that all spiritual forces are brought together so that they can act in concert and in harmony.[11]

The act of creation involved all these spiritual forces acting in concert. Before they could do so, however, a physical point had to be created, which would serve as a focus for all these forces. This was the Foundation Stone, the first point of creation. Since it was the focus of all spiritual forces, it brought them all into play in the creation of the physical universe. It is therefore not surprising to find that the very first word in the Torah — *Bereshyt* — contains an allusion to this spot that was the focus of creation.[12]

It was in this same place that God created man. When God was about to create man, the Torah relates that He said, "Let us make man in our image" (Genesis 1:26). The meaning of this is that God was speaking to all the spiritual forces that He had created, bringing them all into the creation of man, the final

A Jerusalem clothesline with newly laundered woolen tallitot ketanot — a "flag" of loyalty to tradition

Torah study at the Kotel. After services, this man is reviewing the Torah portion of the week.

goal of His creation. In order to bring all these forces to bear upon the creation of man, God created him in the very place where all these forces are focused.[13]

In a dynamic sense, all these forces are actually concentrated in man himself, and this is the meaning of the teaching that man is a microcosm.[14] But man would multiply and become many, while these forces would have to be focused on a single stationary place. Jerusalem, and particularly the Foundation Stone, is therefore a place of gathering, first only for the Jewish people, but ultimately for all mankind. As all men return to their spiritual source, they tend to strengthen the spiritual concentration in this place.[15]

The sages teach that God created man from the place of the Great Altar, the place of his atonement [16] The meaning of this is that the sacrifices, brought on the Altar, would ultimately atone for man's sins. This, however, can also be understood in light of the above. The entire concept of sin is one of spiritual separation, where spiritual forces are separated from each other, and where man is thus separated from God.[17] The concept of sacrifice, on

Using his arms and head, a porter delivers a tray of freshly-baked pita bread in Machaneh Yehudah, Jerusalem's large, teeming market

the other hand, is to reunite these forces, thus bringing man back to God. Indeed, for this reason, the Hebrew word for sacrifice, *Korban*, comes from the root *Karav*, meaning to "be close."[18] But sacrifice and atonement would be accomplished primarily in close proximity to this Foundation Stone, which is the one point that unifies and brings together all spiritual forces. Indeed, the primary purpose of the entire Temple Service was to rectify and strengthen the bond between these forces.

Upon this Foundation Stone stood the Ark, containing the Two Tablets upon which God had written the Ten Commandments, as well as the Original Torah written by Moses. This was to underscore the fact that all creation is sustained by the Covenant of the Torah, as God said, "If not for My covenant day and night, I would not have appointed the decrees of heaven and earth" (Jeremiah 33:25).[19] All creation was contingent upon this covenant, which was made when Israel accepted the Torah from God.[20] The fact that the Ark stood on the Foundation Stone of creation means that all creation is infused with the power of the Torah.

Since this spot is where all spiritual forces come together to

Weighing nuts in Machaneh Yehudah. The sign behind the shopkeeper declares that tithes have been separated as prescribed by the Halachah.

influence the physical world, this is indeed the "Gate of heaven." It is from this spot — between the two Cherubim on the Ark — that prophecy emanates, and through there all prayers are channeled. This spot is the focus of all spiritual forces, and all communication that we have with these forces is through this location. It is thus taught that spiritual channels emanate from the Foundation Stone, bringing spiritual sustenance to all the world.[21]

This also explains the meaning of Jacob's dream, where he saw "a ladder standing on the earth, with its head reaching the heaven" (Genesis 28:12). The concept of a ladder is that of a single entity in which many steps are united. There are many steps on a ladder, but they are all connected by the body of the ladder itself. The same is true of the Foundation Stone, the place where Jacob slept. This too was a single entity to which all spiritual levels are attached.[22]

Since the Foundation Stone unites all spiritual forces, there must be a realm in the spiritual domain where all these forces come together. In the words of our sages, this realm is called "Jerusalem on High," and is said to parallel the physical Jerusalem.[23] This supernal Jerusalem is the realm where all spiritual forces are

Whistle in mouth, with white sleeves for maximum visibility, a policeman carries out the almost impossible task of unclogging the flow of traffic

***Opposite:** The busiest street in the Geulah neighborhood, in front of its busiest pharmacy*

brought together to interact. In the words of some of our sages, this "Jerusalem on High" is called Shalem, from the root *Shalom*, since this is where even opposing spiritual forces exist together in harmony.[24]

As Creator of all spiritual forces, God Himself is infinitely higher than even the highest of them. The difference between God and any created entity, even the highest, is infinitely greater than the difference between even the very highest and very lowest things in creation. God is the Creator, while everything else is created, and there can be no greater fundamental difference than this.

This, however, presents some very serious difficulties. If God is utterly different from all spiritual forces, how can they have any association with Him? We know that God constantly acts upon these forces, this being the entire mechanism of Divine Providence.[25] Furthermore, like everything else, these constantly depend on God for existence itself — if God did not constantly infuse them with His creative force, they would instantly cease to exist.[26] But if both God and these forces are spiritu-

PHARMA
GUEOUL
HOMEOPATHY
J-P HEYMANN
הומאו

A panoramic view of East Jerusalem's most famous landmarks

Opposite: *The Shiloah Pool, ancient aqueduct that brought water to the city*

al and different, then they are separated to the ultimate degree. It would only be through a physical entity that the two could be united.

In many places, when speaking of the Chosen City, the Torah calls it, "The place that God will choose to make His Name dwell there."[27] To the extent that we can understand it, this means that God associates Himself with this place. This is very difficult for the human mind to comprehend, and indeed, Solomon, the wisest of all men, found it impossible to understand. He thus said to God, "Behold the heavens and the heavens of heaven cannot contain You, how much less this house that I have built" (I Kings 8:27). Yet, he knew that God had somehow associated Himself with this place, as God himself had proclaimed in His Torah.[28]

But if both God and the entire array of spiritual forces are associated with this spot — the Foundation Stone — then they can indeed interact. Thus, it is by associating with the Temple and this Stone that God also associates with all the spiritual forces that He created, sustaining and directing them. As mentioned above, however, the array of spiritual forces is called "Jerusalem on High."[29]

We thus see that God does not associate with "Jerusalem on High" until He does so with the physical Jerusalem. This is the meaning of the Talmudic teaching, "God swore that He would not enter Jerusalem on High until He enters Jerusalem down below."[30]

This is also the meaning of the fact that God Himself appeared at the top of the ladder in Jacob's dream. This is the concept of unification, not only affecting all spiritual levels, but also attaching them to God Himself.

The entire purpose of the Temple service was to strengthen this bond between God and the spiritual forces, thus enhancing them and giving them greater power to elevate the physical world. For example, on the festival of Succot, 70 sacrifices were brought, one for each of the 70 archetypal nations of the world.[31] Through this, the directing angels overseeing these nations would be elevated, and, as a result, the nations themselves would be brought to a higher spiritual level.

In a similar manner, other aspects of the Temple service served to enhance other spiritual aspects of humanity. Since the time that the Temple was destroyed, these spiritual aspects have also diminished.

This also explains why all our prayers are directed toward the Foundation Stone, the place of the Ark. We do not pray to any spiritual force or entity, even the highest, but only to God alone. The content of our prayer, however, is to rectify the various spiritual forces, bringing God's light to shine upon them.[32] Since the main connection between God and the spiritual forces is the place of the Ark, we focus our prayers toward this spot.

Through this, we can understand another very difficult Talmudic teaching:[33]

> Rabbi Yochanan said in the name of Rabbi Yosi (ben Zimra): How do we know that God prays? It is written, "I will bring them to My holy mountain, and make them rejoice in the house of My prayer [for My house is a house of prayer for all nations]"(Isaiah 56:7). The Scripture does not say "their prayer," but "My prayer." We thus see that God prays.
>
> And what is His prayer?
>
> Rav Zutra bar Tovia said in the name of Rav: It is, "May it be My will that My mercy should overcome My anger, and that My mercy dominate My Attributes. May I act toward My children with the Attribute of Mercy, and go beyond the requirements of the law."

At first thought this appears beyond all comprehension. How can we say that God prays? And if He does, to whom does He pray? And what is the precise meaning of His prayer?

But if we look carefully at the basic concept of prayer, this becomes somewhat easier to understand. When we pray, the object of our prayer is to bring God's spiritual Light to bear on the spiritual forces, so that they in turn should enhance the world in which we live. Prayer is therefore the enhancement and elevation of the spiritual forces. Of course, the One Who enhances these forces is none other than God Himself, infusing them with His Light and creative force. When God acts upon these forces in this manner, He is said to be "praying."

This also explains the content of God's prayer. The concept of God's anger and His Attribute of Justice is essentially when He withdraws His Light from the spiritual forces, allowing them to function on their own. These forces then function almost automatically, dispensing justice according to a strict rule, in an almost mechanical fashion. This is the idea of God's "hiding His face."[34]

The concept of God's Mercy, on the other hand, is when God makes His Light shine on these forces, taking complete control

Opposite: *The tunnel along the Kotel, below the streets of East Jerusalem. At the* ***top*** *is what is assumed to be an ancient store supplying animals for offerings.* ***Below*** *is a view of a long-buried section of Kotel.*

Above: *"The Kotel has ears" — so the saying goes. Here it listens to the constant prayers of its sons and daughters.*

The remains of an ancient olivepress at Nebi Samuel, the Tomb of the Prophet Samuel

of them, as it were. Thus, when God prays that His Mercy should dominate His Attributes, it means that He is infusing these Attributes with His Light and creative force. This is the concept of God praying.

It is important to note that God's prayer is associated with the Temple in Jerusalem — "For My house is the house of My prayer." According to what we have said earlier, however, the reason for this is obvious. God's prayer refers to His infusing all Attributes and spiritual forces with His Light, which takes place through the Foundation Stone, the focus of all prayer.

It is also very significant to note the ending of this verse, "For My house is a house of prayer to all nations." Here again, at first thought, it is difficult to see what connection this has to God's prayer. Why is the verse that teaches the concept of God's prayer associated with that of the Temple being a place of prayer for all peoples?

We must realize that the main reason there is distinction between Jew and gentile is because of the withholding of God's Light. As a result of the sins of Adam, of the generation of the Flood, and of the builders of the Tower of Babel, God gradually withdrew His Light from the world, restricting it to one people, the Jews, who would inhabit Jerusalem and serve God there.[35] Therefore, there are directing angels over the gentile nations, but they are on a lower level than the spiritual forces associated with Israel.[36]

The concept of God's prayer, however, is that His Light should shine through all spiritual forces with its full intensity, and thus, to all mankind as well. Therefore, when God's house is the "house of His prayer," it is then also "a house of prayer for all nations."[37]

This again brings us to the location of the Foundation Stone, the focus of all spiritual forces. It was set on the crossroads of civilization, so that all peoples should interact with these forces and, throughout history, be influenced by them. In this manner, all mankind is gradually elevated by these forces, paving the way for the ultimate rectification of the world. This will be realized in the Messianic Age, when Jerusalem becomes a center for God's teaching for all mankind: "Out of Zion shall come forth the Torah, and God's word from Jerusalem."

Focus of a People

One of the Old City's countless alleyways

Imagine yourself in Jerusalem two thousand years ago. It is the festival of Passover, and Jews from all over the world are coming to celebrate the holy season. They come from every direction, first by hundreds, then by thousands, and finally by hundreds of thousands. When the festival arrives, a good portion of the entire Jewish population is concentrated in this one city. As far as the eye can see, the mountain slopes are covered with tents, where people will roast their paschal lamb, which in the time of the Temple was the focal point of the Passover service.

As the Torah prescribes, the paschal lamb can be prepared only in one place: "You shall sacrifice the Passover offering to the Lord your God ... in the place that God shall choose to make His Name dwell there" (Deuteronomy 16:2). The Torah states that God would choose a place, and that it would be the only place in the world where such an offering could be made. And

The Old City and the Jerusalem hills, with the Temple Mount in the foreground

what was true of the Passover offering was true of many other important aspects of Jewish life. According to the rule set down by the Torah, these rituals could be observed only in "the place that God would choose."[1] This "place" was Jerusalem.

For almost a thousand years, from the time that it was dedicated by King David until it was destroyed by the Romans, Jerusalem was the focal point of the Jewish people.[2] There were certain things that could only be accomplished in Jerusalem; no matter where a Jew lived, he would have to go to this holy city to do these things. Since there were so many rituals that could be performed only in Jerusalem, our sages teach us that "Jerusalem is more holy than the rest of the Land of Israel."[3]

Among the most dramatic of these observances were the three annual pilgrimages. There are three festivals, Succot, Passover, and Shavuot, during which, in the days of the Temple, the Torah required every Jew who was able to, to make a pilgrimage to "the place chosen by God." The Torah thus states, "Three times a year shall all your males appear before the Lord your God in the place which He shall choose, on the feast of

The wall around the Old City.
At the right foreground is a group of artists' studios and shop. At the foot of the wall is a series of archeological excavations.

Matzot (Passover), on the feast of Shavuot, and on the feast of Succot" (Deuteronomy 16:16).

During these pilgrimages, Jews poured into Jerusalem from all over the world. They renewed friendships and exchanged news. As a result, the Jews were united and molded into a single people.[4] But most important, all this was done within a context of holiness and serving God. The fact that so many people were gathering in worship would reinforce all of them religiously and morally, so much so that in the course of these pilgrimages, no Jew would be suspected of harming another in any way.[5] Thus, Jerusalem united the Jewish people in a context that directed this unity toward the unity of God.

This helps us to understand why the "place chosen by God" had to be a city. What is a city? Besides a mere concentration of people, it is a place where civilization grows and develops. The very concentration of people in a city results in an exchange and growth of ideas. It is therefore not coincidence that the growth of civilization in general has historically emanated from its cities. While the farmlands provided food for the body, the cities provided food for the mind and soul. As Rabbi Samson

The Machne Yehuda market — always a busy place

Raphael Hirsch points out, the Hebrew word for city, *Ir* (עיר), comes from the same base as the word *Ur* (עור), meaning "to awaken."[6] It is the city that awakens mankind, bringing out his best creative instincts. Indeed, in the Torah we find that the building of cities led to many of the most important developments in civilization.[7]

The focal point of Jewish civilization was to develop a relationship with God; and this too required a city. Jerusalem became the place where Jews from all over the world would gather to exchange ideas and develop a civilization enhancing this relationship. Vital to this process were the Temple and the many teachers of Torah who lived in Jerusalem, which will be discussed in a further chapter. But in general, it was Jerusalem that was the city — the "awakener" — arousing and motivating the Jew toward his mission. It is not very surprising that our sages teach that Jerusalem is the highest realization of the concept of the City.[8]

A typical highway sign — in three languages, of course

This is seen very explicitly also with respect to the "Second Tithe" (*Maaser Sheni*). There were a number of tithes from all crops grown in the Holy Land, that had to be given as a kind of income tax to support the *Cohanim*-Priests and Levites, who served as religious leaders and teachers. One-tenth of all produce grown in the Holy Land was the tithe given to the Levites, while a smaller portion, known as Terumah, was given to the *Cohen*-Priest.

In addition, there was the Second Tithe.[9] This was not given away; instead, the owner himself had either to eat it in Jerusalem, or redeem it and spend the money for food in Jerusalem. Here, the Torah itself provides a reason: "You shall eat before the Lord your God in the place that He shall choose for His Name to dwell, the tithe of your corn, wine and oil ... that you may learn always to fear the Lord your God"(Deuteronomy 14:23).

Instead of giving this tithe to the Priest and Levite, the owner himself would become a "Priest and Levite" while living off this tithe in Jerusalem.[10] He would have to take time off from his usual occupation, purify himself in the prescribed manner, and remain in Jerusalem until the tithe was consumed. If he could not go himself, he would send his children to Jerusalem to live off the tithe. In this manner, either he or his children would be exposed to the atmosphere of Jerusalem, to the worship and intellectual ferment that filled the air; and they would be able to grow and develop in the ways of the Torah. In this manner the ideal would be fulfilled, wherein the entire Jewish people would become "a kingdom of priests and a holy nation"(Exodus 19:6). The system of the "Second Tithe" insured that every Jew would spend at least a part of the year as a resident of Jerusalem, and

The magnificent stained glass windows above the Holy Ark of the Heichal Shlomo Synagogue

this would be a period of spiritual regeneration for all members of the Jewish people.[11]

There were many other observances that could be kept only in the "place chosen by God," that is, in Jerusalem. There was a tithe of all livestock that had to be eaten in the Holy City.[12] The First Fruits had to be brought to the "place that God will choose," involving a meaningful ceremony.[13] These practices served the important purpose of causing each and every Jew to make regular visits to Jerusalem, thus experiencing the spiritual renewal and unifying influence associated with this city.

Most of these practices affected only Jews living in the Holy Land. There were other commandments, however, that affected Jews wherever they lived. These involved the system of sacrifices. In the Torah, particularly at the beginning of Leviticus, a number of sacrifices are prescribed. Some can be brought as a free will offering, but the most common reason for the offering of a sacrifice was the atonement of a sin.

According to the Ramban (*Nachmanides*), the primary purpose of the sacrifice was that by being involved in the slaughter of an animal, the person bringing it would also experience vicarious death. When the *Cohen*-Priest slaughtered the animal and burned it on the Altar, the person bringing it would feel as though he himself had been killed and burned for having gone against the word of God.[14] Furthermore, God gave man the power of intellect so that he would be able to perfect himself. When a person sins, it is as if he has rejected his God-given intellect. Since the main thing distinguishing man from the animals is his intellect, when a person sins he is actually identifying with the animals. For this reason, an animal must be sacrificed.[15]

On a deeper level, man consists of two elements, the animal and the divine; and these two elements are in constant conflict with each other.[16] While the divine in man pulls him toward the spiritual, the animal in him draws him toward the physical and the mundane. When a person sins, he must therefore bring an animal as a sacrifice. By being an offering to God, the animal itself is elevated; at the same time, the animal in man, which can identify with this animal being sacrificed, is also elevated. The animal in man, which caused him to sin, is then brought back under the subjugation of the divine.[17]

The Istanbul Synagogue in the Old City

All of these reasons merely touch the surface of the concept of sacrifices, which involves some of the deepest ideas of Judaism. It is obvious that the entire sacrificial system would appear brutal and barbaric unless administered in an almost perfect religious atmosphere. Only a nation of the highest moral and spiritual caliber could be worthy of it. Therefore, because of the moral laxity and spiritual degeneration of the Jewish people, the sacrificial system was eventually abolished.[18]

Sacrifices could be offered only in one place, the Holy Temple (*Bet HaMikdash*) in Jerusalem. This is explicitly prescribed in the Torah: "God shall choose a place for His Name to

Two noteworthy buildings just outside the Old City walls, the Diaspora Yeshiva ***(top);*** *the Bustenai Building (****bottom)***

Across: *The Jaffa Gate, one of the main entrances to the Old City*

dwell; there shall you bring your offerings and sacrifices, your tithes and gifts" (Deuteronomy 12:11). Ever since the Temple was built in Jerusalem, in no other place in the world can sacrifices be offered.

It is considered a most serious sin to offer a sacrifice outside the Jerusalem Temple.[19] Here again, the reason is that it must be done in a place of the utmost holiness, so that the sacrificial system will not degenerate into something barbaric and brutal. The author of the *Sefer HaChinuch* writes that killing an animal wantonly, if not done for food or in the proper worship of God in the proper place, is an act of murder.[20] In this manner, the sacrificial system actually taught us to respect all life, even that of an animal. The severest penalties were invoked against a person who killed an animal as a sacrifice, not in a place of holiness and according to the prescribed law.

There was therefore a commandment that a person bringing a sacrifice must be actively involved in bringing it to the Temple in Jerusalem, as the Torah states, "You shall take the holy things that you have and your vow-offerings, and go to the place that God will choose" (Deuteronomy 12:26).[21] Beyond this, it was important that every individual be physically present to place his hands on his sacrifice before it was offered. One could send his sacrifice to Jerusalem through an agent or messenger, but the latter could not perform the ritual of laying the hands on the offering. The sacrifice might be valid without this laying of hands, but the atonement was not complete.[22] The actual offering of the sacrifice, of course, could be done only by a *Cohen*-Priest.

Thus, whenever a person committed a sin requiring a sacrifice, he was virtually compelled to make a pilgrimage to Jerusalem to seek atonement. There was a particular significance in the fact that one had to make this pilgrimage. In sinning, the person demonstrated that his relationship to God was not perfect and complete; therefore, he would have to visit Jerusalem to strengthen this relationship. Only in Jerusalem could he once again become spiritually whole, renewing his commitment so as to avoid future sin.

The Temple was destroyed by the Romans in the year 68 C. E. and since then, sacrifices are no longer offered. People sin so often today that if they had to bring a sacrifice for each offense, everyone would be bringing an offering daily. In the *Nèillah* service on Yom Kippur, we say, "there is no end of the offerings required of us, countless would be our guilt sacrifices." As mentioned earlier, this is actually one reason why

the sacrificial system had to be abolished. Today we make up for the lack of sacrifices with prayer and Torah study, as the prophet said, "We shall render for bullocks the offerings of our lips" (Hosea 14:3).[23]

From all this we learn a most important lesson. The fact that a single city was central to Judaism is not an accident. In many places, the Torah mentions such a central city — the "place that God will choose" — and mandates many practices that will obligate the Jew to make periodic pilgrimages to this place. God knew that if the Jewish people were to be molded into a people worthy of fulfilling their mission, they would have to have such a center as its focus.

Although most of these practices are no longer observed, Jerusalem still retains its status as a focal point of Judaism. God Himself determined that Jerusalem would be the holy city; and something so prescribed by God cannot be retracted. Thus, the status of Jerusalem as a holy city exists even to this day.[24] God considers it necessary that such a focal point exist even today. Jerusalem still serves as a focus of the Jewish people, as well as a central point of their mission.

Bargain hunting in the Bucharan market

The Temple

Entrance to the Zion Gate of the city wall

If Jerusalem was the focal point of the Land of Israel, it was the Temple (*Bet HaMikdash*) that was the focal point of Jerusalem. The first Temple was built by King Solomon. It stood for 410 years until it was destroyed by Nebuchadnezzar and the Babylonians. Seventy years later, the second Temple was built by Ezra. According to tradition, it stood for 420 years, until it was razed by the Roman legions under Titus.[1]

Many people think of the Jerusalem Temple as being some kind of synagogue, but it was actually a unique structure. Shortly after the Exodus from Egypt, God commanded the Israelites to build a Tabernacle (*Mishkan*) in the desert.[2] God said, “They shall make for Me a sanctuary, and I will dwell inside them” (Exodus 25:8). The commentaries note that the verse does not say, “I will dwell inside it,” but rather, “inside them.” Through this Tabernacle, God's presence would dwell in the heart of each and every Jew.[3]

Plaza in front of the famed Hurva Synagogue in the Old City, which was destroyed under Jordanian occupation

One can obtain an idea of the importance of the Tabernacle from the fact that almost the entire second half of the Book of Exodus is devoted to its description and building. To some extent, we can understand its significance from the teaching that this Tabernacle was meant to be a microcosm of all creation.[4] As such it was meant to teach man that he has a responsibility to elevate and sanctify all creation. The Tabernacle represented man's partnership with God in bringing the world toward its final goal; thus, in a sense, the building of the Tabernacle paralleled God's own act of Creation.[5]

The Tabernacle was a most remarkable building, all the more so since it was probably the world's first prefabricated structure. Although it was rather large, some 20-feet high, 24-feet wide, and 64-feet long, the entire structure could be taken apart and transported from place to place. The Tabernacle thus accompanied the Israelites throughout their period of wandering in the desert. Even after they entered the Holy Land, it was occasionally moved from place to place. According to Biblical tradition, it stood in Gilgal for14 years, in

The living room of a Cohen's residence — from the Herodian period

Shiloh for 369 years, and eventually in Nob and then in Gibeon for a total of 57 years.[6]

Besides the general commandment to build a sanctuary, there was also a commandment that a permanent Temple be built, as the Torah states, "You shall seek [God's] habitation"(Deuteronomy 12:5).[7] This could not be accomplished until after the Israelites had occupied the Promised Land, appointed a king, and attained a state of peace with the neighboring lands. The Torah thus continues, "When you cross the Jordan, dwelling in the land which the Lord your God gives you to inherit, and He gives you rest from all your enemies round about so that you dwell in safety; then there shall be the place which the Lord your God will choose to make His Name dwell there" (Deuteronomy 12:10,11). Such peace was not attained until the time of David and Solomon; therefore, only then could the place be chosen and the Temple built.[8]

One of the important features of the Temple was the Great Altar (*Mizbèach*) upon which all sacrifices were offered. As discussed earlier, this Altar was the only place in the world where a sacrifice could be offered to God.

It is interesting to note that to this very day, a central platform, called a *Bimah* or *Almemar*, is built in the synagogue. On this platform the Torah is read. This platform parallels the Great Altar, which was located in the center of the Jerusalem Temple. On the festival of Succot, we march around this platform, just as people once marched around the Great Altar of the Temple.[9]

The Temple also had an inner chamber called the *Hechal*, containing three main features. The best known of these was the golden Menorah, a huge seven-branched candelabrum, taller than a man. Six of the seven lamps on this Menorah were kindled each evening, while the middle lamp burned constantly as the Eternal Light.[10] This was the Menorah that played a key role in the miracle of Chanukah during the time of the Second Temple.

Besides the Menorah, this inner chamber contained a golden altar for incense and a special table upon which the show-bread was placed.[11]

Past this chamber was the Holy of Holies, the innermost chamber and the focal point of the Temple. So great was the

Organized pandemonium — the Central Bus Terminal. Soldiers and civilians, shoppers and commuters, a busy country ready to fill its roads.

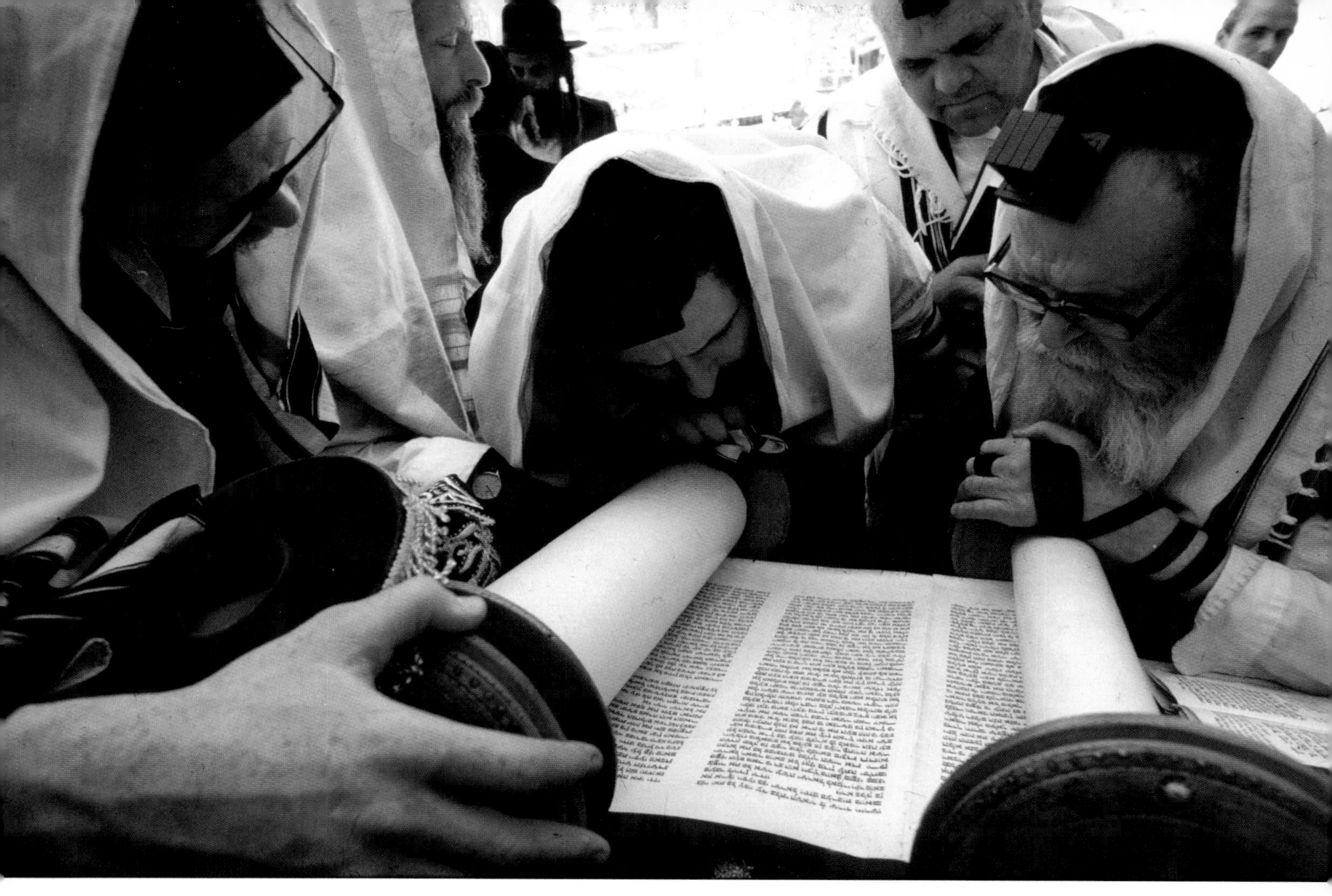
Torah reading at the Kotel

holiness of this chamber that no person was ever allowed to enter it, other than the High Priest (*Cohen Gadol*) and only on Yom Kippur. This was part of a most impressive service. Jews from all over the world would gather in Jerusalem to see the High Priest emerge in peace after having worshiped in this inner sanctuary.[12] Even today, one of the most dramatic portions of the Yom Kippur service is the portion in the Mussaf which recounts how the High Priest would enter the Holy of Holies.

In the center of the Holy of Holies stood the Ark of the Covenant, which was made of wood covered with gold. On this Ark was a cover of pure gold, and attached to this cover were the two gold Cherubim. The entire structure of the Ark, its cover and the Cherubim are described in detail in the Torah, and they were made under the personal supervision of Moses.[13]

But even more important was the Ark's contents. For in it were the objects that were most sacred to Judaism: the two Tablets inscribed with the Ten Commandments, which God had given to Moses, and the original Torah that Moses himself had written as dictated by God.[14]

A soldier checking the bag of a girl coming to pray at the Kotel — one of the unpleasant but necessary aspects of the constant concern with security

Opposite: *A bullet-pocked entrance in the city wall*

When King Solomon built the Temple, he constructed a deep labyrinth going under the Temple Mount, where the holy vessels could be hidden in case of danger. Foreseeing that Jerusalem would be threatened, King Josiah commanded that the Ark be concealed in this labyrinth, sealing it off so that it would not be discovered by the enemy. Thus, even to this day, the Ark is hidden somewhere under the Temple Mount in Jerusalem.[15]

This is a most important point. The single most significant event in Jewish history was the revelation at Sinai, when God Himself proclaimed the Ten Commandments. It was at this time that God made the covenant establishing His unique relationship with His people Israel. In some places, these Tablets are known as "the Tablets of the covenant," indicating that they contain the words of the covenant made at Sinai.[16] Elsewhere, they are called "the Tablets of testimony," since they are a permanent, tangible testimony to the existence of this covenant.[17] The Tablets represent the physical reality of the covenant, the special relationship between God and the Jewish people.

No less central to Judaism is the Torah as a whole. In general, a scroll of the Torah is the most sacred object of the Jew. If

this is true of *any* Torah scroll, how much more so is it true of the original Torah, written by Moses at the expressed word of God! This unique Torah was written by Moses shortly before he died, and he commanded that it be placed in the Ark, next to the Tablets: "Take this book of the Torah, and put it in the side of the Ark of the covenant of the Lord your God, that it may be there as a witness for you" (Deuteronomy 31:24). Moses' Torah was thus placed in the Ark, right next to the Tablets of the covenant. As Rambam (*Maimonides*) writes, this is the "witness" to all mankind of the special relationship and responsibility that we have to God.[18]

Even though the Ark, the Tablets and the original Torah were not on display, every Jew coming to Jerusalem knew that he was in close proximity to these most sacred objects.[19] He might meditate on the covenant, mentally going back to the revelation at Sinai, contemplating all the miracles that accompanied the giving of the Torah.

A street sweeper designed for the narrow streets of Jerusalem's older neighborhoods

Even today, it is possible to experience this feeling of proximity. These most sacred objects still remain hidden in Jerusalem, buried deep in a vault under the Temple Mount. Here they will remain until the time when we are worthy to uncover them once again. And even though we may not actually be aware of these sacred objects, the very fact of their proximity is sure to make a most profound impression on our souls.

One remnant of the Temple still stands today. This is the Western Wall of the Temple Mount, the *Kotel Maaravi*. To this day, it is considered one of the most sacred spots in the world; it is the focus of pilgrimage for Jews from all over. Our sages teach us that even though the Temple was destroyed, the Divine Presence never left the Western Wall.[20] The Western Wall is special, since it was the wall that was closest to the Holy of Holies.

The Sanhedrin

Mea Shearim — the neighborhood of One Hundred Gates

"Out of Zion shall go forth the Torah, and the Word of God from Jerusalem" (Isaiah 2:3). Jerusalem was more than a place where people gathered; it was also a place from which teaching emanated. As the prophet so aptly puts it, Zion and Jerusalem were the main places where the Torah was taught, guiding Jews wherever they might live. It is the Torah that makes the Jew what he is; it directs the life of the entire Jewish nation. Jerusalem was the center of the interpretation and teaching of the Torah.[1]

Built into the outer north wall of the Temple, not far from the Great Altar, was a room known as the Chamber of Cut Stone. In this chamber the great Sanhedrin sat, teaching and judging all Israel.[2]

The establishment of this Sanhedrin as well as other judicial bodies, to interpret and decide questions of Torah law, was decreed by the Torah: "Judges and officers shall you appoint in

Tombs of the Sanhedrin, dating from the Second Temple era, in the Sanhedria neighborhood

all your gates, that God will give you" (Deuteronomy 16:18). The primary obligation implied by this commandment was to set up and support such a duly ordained Sanhedrin.[3] This Sanhedrin consisted of seventy-one men, chosen from the greatest sages of Israel. This is learned from God's commandment to Moses, "Gather to Me seventy elders of Israel... and bring them to the Tent of Meeting, that they may stand there with you" (Numbers 11:16). According to tradition, this was the first Sanhedrin, and since Moses himself must be counted as its head, it is obvious that it consisted of seventy-one members.[4]

The "Tent of Meeting" (*Ohel Moed*) in this verse refers to the Tabernacle in the desert, which, as discussed in the previous chapter, had its counterpart in the Holy Temple in Jerusalem.[5] Thus, when God told Moses to "bring them to the Tent of Meeting," this is an allusion that the Sanhedrin must convene in close proximity to the Temple. There are numerous other allusions teaching that the Sanhedrin must be near the Great Altar.[6]

Every member of the Sanhedrin had to be distinguished in wisdom, humility, fear of God, disdain for monetary gain, a passion for truth, and love for his fellow man, as well as outstanding expertise in all areas of Torah scholarship. Regarding their selection, the Torah thus states, "You shall search from among all the people, able men, who fear God, men of truth, disdaining unjust gain, and you shall place [these men] over [the people]" (Exodus 18:21). Moses, too, told the people, "Take from each of your tribes men who are wise, understanding and full of knowledge, and I will make them leaders over you" (Deuteronomy 1:13).[7]

Another view of the tombs of the Sanhedrin

The Sanhedrin was in existence from the time of Moses until it was disbanded after the destruction of Jerusalem by the Romans.[8] As long as the Sanhedrin convened, it functioned as both the supreme court and the central legislative body for all Israel. As a supreme court, it was the final authority in all matters of Torah law; any case that could not be judged adequately by a lower court was brought to it.[9] As a legislature, the Sanhedrin had the authority to enact religious laws that would be binding on all Israel. This authority was given to it by the Torah itself, as it is written, "According to the law that they teach you ... you shall do" (Deuteronomy 17:11). Any legislation enacted by the Sanhedrin is called a Rabbinical Law, as distinguished from a Torah Law.[10]

The most important function of the Sanhedrin, however, was the preservation, interpretation, and teaching of the Oral Torah.[11]

The new Municipal Building of the city of Jerusalem

The Torah that God gave Moses actually consisted of two parts, the written and the oral. The Written Torah was the original Torah scroll written by Moses, which was copied and recopied with the greatest accuracy, insuring that the Torah we read today is identical with that transmitted by God. The Oral Torah consisted of all the explanations and interpretations surrounding the Written Torah, as well as many laws given to Moses by God which were never written down. Since the Written Torah is sometimes ambiguous, and often omits important details, it can be kept adequately only through the Oral Tradition.

There are numerous cases where the Torah refers to details not included in the written text, implying that there was an oral tradition. For example, when the Torah speaks of kosher ritual slaughter, it states, "You shall slaughter your cattle ... as I have commanded you" (Deuteronomy 12:21), alluding to an oral commandment.[12] Similarly, the Torah speaks of such commandments as the Sabbath, Tefillin, and Tzitzith, and since no details are supplied, it must be assumed that they are included in the Oral Torah.[13]

The need for such an Oral Torah should be obvious. The

Jerusalem's Central Bus Station, a primary hub of the nation's public transportation system

Torah was not meant to be merely a book, lying on the shelf. It was intended to be the main motivating force in the daily lives of an entire people. As such it could only be transmitted by word of mouth, entrusted to a body of elders who would interpret it according to the needs of the time. This Oral Torah was handed down from teacher to disciple for almost fifteen hundred years, from the time of Moses until after the Romans destroyed Jerusalem. During this entire period, the tradition was preserved by the Sanhedrin. Only after the Sanhedrin was exiled and finally disbanded was the Oral Torah written down to form the Talmud and Midrash.

In many respects, the Oral Law is seen as being even more important than its written counterpart. In one place, the Talmud teaches that the Oral Torah is more dear to God than the Written Torah.[14] It is, furthermore, taught that the main covenant God made with Israel was based on the Oral, not the Written Torah.[15] While the Tablets and the written scroll testified to the existence of the covenant, it was the Oral Torah that taught how to live by it.

Jerusalem was the center of both parts of the Torah, the Written and the Oral. As discussed earlier, both the Tablets and

Shaar Shechem, the Damascus Gate, the primary entrance to the Moslem Quarter

the original Torah scroll written by Moses were kept in the Ark, in the Holy of Holies. And the Oral Torah was entrusted to the Sanhedrin, only a short distance away.[16]

As in the case of the Temple itself, the Torah prescribes that the Sanhedrin be located in "the place chosen by God." The Torah states, "When there arises a matter too hard for you to judge ... within your gates, you shall rise and go up to the place that the Lord your God shall choose. And you shall go to the priests, the Levites, and the Judge who shall exist in those days, and you shall inquire, and they shall declare to you the word of judgment" (Deuteronomy 17:8, 9). Just as the Temple had to be in the place chosen by God, so did the Sanhedrin.

It is important to note that only from the commandment regarding the Sanhedrin have we an allusion as to where this chosen place would be. In speaking of the Sanhedrin, the Torah states, "you shall ... go up to the place," indicating that the chosen place would be in one of the highest elevations in the Promised Land.[17] As mentioned earlier, the Sanhedrin had to be in close proximity to the Altar, so this also defined the place

A sight that has become pleasantly familiar in recent years. A bar mitzvah at the Kotel of a youngster from Ethiopia.

of the Temple. Indeed, we find that King David and the Prophet Samuel used this verse when they attempted to determine the place chosen by God.[18]

The fact that the chosen place is determined by the location of the Sanhedrin appears to indicate that the primary reason such a place had to exist was for the sake of this body. As discussed earlier, one of the main functions of the Temple was educational — "That you may learn always to fear the Lord your God" (Deuteronomy 14:23). But if such education was the goal, the main source of such education indeed was the Sanhedrin, who taught the Torah to all Israel. If unification of the Jewish nation was the goal, then again the Sanhedrin was of central importance. The main unifying force among the Jewish people was the Torah; since a single body — the Sanhedrin — would interpret and teach it, all Jews, no matter where they lived, would keep it in the same manner. Nothing united the Jews more than this, so the Torah says, "There shall be one Torah for you" (Numbers 15:16).[19] Furthermore, even today, over nineteen hundred years after the destruction of the Temple, the influ-

ence of the Sanhedrin still plays a dominant role in the religious life of the Jew, no matter where he lives.

The room in which the Sanhedrin convened was called the *Lishkat HaGazit*, the Chamber of Cut Stones. This was a chamber built in the wall of the Temple, half inside the sanctuary and half outside, with doors providing access both to the Temple and to the outside. The place where the Sanhedrin actually convened was outside of the sanctuary area, since the members sat while in judgment, and it is forbidden to sit inside the sanctuary area.[20] If there were no entrance from the outside, people would have to go through the Temple in order to come to the Sanhedrin; and it is forbidden to make use of the Temple to go to someplace outside the sanctuary area.[21]

On the other hand, part of this chamber had to be inside the sanctuary area, since the Sanhedrin judged many things involving the priests and the Temple service, which had to be done within the Temple grounds.[22] Furthermore, questions would often arise in the midst of the divine service, and at such times, it was forbidden for a priest to leave the sanctuary area.[23] Also the requirement that the Sanhedrin be near the Altar meant that there had to be direct access from the Altar to the Sanhedrin.[24]

The reason why this chamber was built into the north wall is not defined, but several points come to mind. The members of the Sanhedrin could not sit with their backs to the Temple, so, when they sat facing the Temple, they faced toward the south. The Talmud teaches that facing in this direction has the potential to inspire wisdom.[25] In a mystical sense, the north is associated with judgment, which is the main task of the Sanhedrin.[26]

The reason why this chamber in particular is said to be built of cut stone is also not clear. Here, however, there is a clear contrast to the Altar, of which the Torah states, "You shall *not* build it of cut stones" (Exodus 20:22). For this reason the stones for the Altar had to be dug up from deep in the ground, or taken from the depths of the sea, where they could not possibly have come in contact with human tools.[27]

The reason for this is that the cutting and shaping of stones is a human activity, based on man's intellectual ability, as distinguished from his animal nature. The Altar, as discussed earlier, was meant to rectify man's animal nature, and therefore had to be built entirely of natural stones.

Furthermore, the introduction of man's intellectual nature into the formation of these stones might sully them with his animal nature as well. If the Altar itself were defiled by man's animal nature, it would not be able to rectify this element in man. In forbidding cut stones, the Torah therefore says, "for your sword has been lifted against it to desecrate it" (ibid.). The sword represents the subjugation of man's intellect to his animal nature, because in war man makes use of his intellect to satisfy his animal instincts. This is the precise opposite of the function of the Altar, which was meant to subjugate the animal in man to his Divine element. If man's animal nature were allowed to interject, the entire sacrificial system represented by the Altar would become brutal and barbaric. Therefore, the Altar had to be made of stones as created by God, and not as modified by man.[28]

The Sanhedrin, on the other hand, was meant to teach the Torah, thus rectifying man's Divine nature. The stones of the chamber of the Sanhedrin were especially cut so that they would be the product of man's intellect. Here it was specifically

Opposite: *Two of the oldest neighborhoods in the New City, Yemin Moshe* ***(above)*** *and Bucharim* ***(below)***

Above: *A rare Jerusalem scene: snow on the rooftops of the Beth Israel neighborhood*

demonstrated that there was no fear that man's animal nature, represented by the sword, would interject, because the Torah taught by the Sanhedrin was precisely that which had the power to subjugate man's animal nature. Therefore, unlike the Altar, the hall of the Sanhedrin was made particularly of cut stone.[29]

Since the hall of the Sanhedrin was built of cut stone, we see a sharp contrast between its concept and that of the Altar. While the Altar was directed toward man's animal nature, the Sanhedrin was directed toward his Divine, intellectual nature. While the Altar was meant to rectify the evil in man, the Sanhedrin would enhance the Torah, which was his ultimate good. While the Altar would burn the sacrifice and return it to its natural elements, the Sanhedrin would teach man how to take the world that God created and use it in fulfilling God's purpose.

At David's Tower Museum

Still, as mentioned earlier, there had to be direct access from the Altar to the Sanhedrin. Man is a complex being; only between these two ideals could he be totally rectified and elevated. This entire process was centered in one place — Jerusalem. Another important point is that the Sanhedrin was invested with its full powers only when it sat in this Chamber of Cut Stone. The Torah thus says, "You shall follow the decision that they tell you from the place which God shall choose, and you shall be careful to do like all that they teach you" (Deuteronomy 17:10). The Sanhedrin legally could be convened in any place in the Holy

Land; but if it were not in the Chamber of Cut Stone, its authority and powers were severely limited.[30]

It is also important to note that the hall of the Sanhedrin also served as the synagogue on the Temple grounds, where the daily prayer service was held. [31] The commentaries state that this is because worship is most acceptable before God when conducted in a place where the Torah is taught and studied. For this reason, even today, a Yeshiva where people study the Torah is considered a preferred place for worship.[32]

Inside the Zion Gate

The counterpoint between the Temple and the Sanhedrin may also explain an interesting discussion in the Midrash. The mountain upon which the Temple is built is called Mount Moriah, and there are numerous opinions as to the reason for this name. In the Midrash, two opinions are noted. One states that it indicates awe and fear (*Yirah*); and the other, that it indicates decision and teaching (*Horah*).[33] Fear and awe of God are the main concepts of the Temple itself, as the Torah states, "You shall fear My sanctuary" (Leviticus 19:30, 26:2). Thus, according to one opinion, the main point of Jerusalem was the Temple itself. According to the other opinion, however, the main purpose of this mountain was the teachings and decisions rendered by the Sanhedrin.

The fact that the Sanhedrin was centered in Jerusalem had very important implications for the city itself. It must be remembered that the members of the Sanhedrin were the great-

In the David's Tower Museum

est minds and foremost teachers in the Jewish world. Besides their judicial responsibilities, many members of the Sanhedrin headed important academies, where the Oral Torah was taught and expounded. Disciples by the tens of thousands would flock to Jerusalem to study in its numerous academies, which were the best and most prestigious in the Jewish world. All of this had the effect of making Jerusalem the uncontested intellectual capital of the Jewish people.[34]

A pilgrim coming to Jerusalem would thus be engulfed in a sea of intellectual activity. He could not help but come in contact with the thousands of disciples who filled the streets of Jerusalem; and on occasion, he might even catch a glimpse of the great masters of Torah, the members of the Sanhedrin themselves. A person living in Jerusalem while consuming his Second Tithe would be in such an atmosphere for weeks at a time, and he might even enroll in one of the academies himself. The teachings of the Torah were thus spread throughout the entire Jewish nation, making the Jews a truly holy people, dedicated to God and His teachings.

Kings and Prophets

Dusk in a city of many cultures — a minaret at the Tower of David

Among other things, Jerusalem was the seat of government of the Jewish nation. In Jerusalem, David established his kingdom; as long as there was a central government in Israel, this was its center.

Obviously, if the nation were to be unified, some sort of central government would be necessary. The head of this government was called a king (*melech*), even though his powers were severely limited by the Torah. Once the promised land was occupied and inhabited, the Torah commanded the Jews to appoint a king. "When you come to the land that the Lord your God gives you, possessing it and dwelling in it ... you shall appoint a king over you, whom the Lord your God shall choose" (Deuteronomy 17:14,15). The fact that the Torah says that God must choose the king indicates that he must be chosen with the concurrence of both a prophet and the Sanhedrin.[1]

The power of a Jewish king was far from absolute. Like every other Jew, he was bound by the law of the Torah; in the case of a king, this was emphasized all the more, since the king was required to write his own scroll of the Torah and keep it on his person at all times.[2] In this respect, the government was a constitutional monarchy, with the Torah being its God-given constitution. Similarly, like every other Jew, the king was bound to obey the dictates of the Sanhedrin, so for all practical purposes, he was little more than the chief administrator of the government.[3]

The permanent place "chosen by God" could not be revealed until after a king had been appointed. Furthermore, the site of the Temple, as well as the Holy City surrounding it, had to be dedicated in a special manner, with an involved ceremony. This dedication could only be accomplished when a king, a prophet, and the Sanhedrin were present.[4] Thus, Jerusalem was not chosen to be the Holy City until after David was appointed as king over all Israel. Although it is not explicitly stated, it appears that dedicating this city is the main function of a king; it is actually the only place where the Torah requires the presence of a king.

Opposite: *Prayers at Tomb of Shimon HaTzaddik, a High Priest and member of the Men of the Great Assembly at the beginning of the Second Temple era*

Above: *The Tomb of Kings, burial place of Kings of the Davidic dynasty during the First Temple era*

There was also a tradition that whoever occupied this "place that God would choose" would be the one to initiate the royal line in Israel.[5] In performing the one act where the Torah actually requires a king, this person would define himself as the king mentioned in the Torah. The law then states that this king's children would inherit the kingdom forever, as it is written, "he will prolong the days of his kingdom, him and his children" (Deuteronomy 17:20). The one who becomes king as defined in the Torah therefore sets the royal line for all time. Thus, when David's son Solomon dedicated Jerusalem as the "Chosen Place," the royal line became fixed with the descendants of David forever.[6]

There is a tradition in the Oral Torah that David's royal line would have its seat of government in Jerusalem. It is thus written regarding Jerusalem, "It is there that thrones of justice are set, thrones of the house of David" (Psalms 122:5). The "thrones of justice" refer to the seats of the Sanhedrin, while the "thrones of the house of David" refer to those of the royal line.[7] Besides this, King David himself served as the head of the Sanhedrin in his time; therefore, its headquarters had to be in the same vicinity.[8]

Tombs of the Prophets on the Mount of Olives

Among the most important leaders and teachers of Israel during the period of the First Temple were the prophets. This was still a formative period for the Jewish people. It was through these prophets that God revealed His will, guiding His people along the path that He had chosen for them. Indeed, the Bible consists of three portions, the Torah, the Prophets, and the Writings, and the last two were composed chiefly by the Prophets of Israel.

The Talmud teaches that most of the prophets lived and taught in Jerusalem.[9] According to a number of traditions, most of their prophecies were pronounced in the Hall of the Sanhedrin.[10]

There were a number of important reasons for this. First, not everyone could be recognized as a prophet. Among other things, for a person to be chosen by God as His prophet, an individual would have to be outstanding in piety and knowledge of the Torah.[11] Such an individual would most likely be found among the members of the Sanhedrin, since these were the greatest saints and sages of Israel. Looking at the record, we find that in many cases, the great prophets themselves served as the heads of the Sanhedrin.[12]

Another reason why the prophets had to be in Jerusalem was that a prophet could be accredited and recognized only by the Sanhedrin.[13] No one could simply declare himself a prophet and have himself accepted as a spokesman of God, since to permit this would open the door to any charlatan or demagogue. Before a person could be accepted as a prophet, he would have to provide some unequivocal sign, the most common being an accurate prediction of the future. The Torah thus prescribes, "Should you ask yourselves, 'How can we know that the word was not spoken by God?' If the prophet speaks in the name of God and his word does not come true, then that word was not granted by God, but the prophet spoke it presumptuously" (Deuteronomy 18:21,22).

From this, we also learn the converse, that the way of testing the authenticity of a prophet is to see if he can accurately predict the future. If a person otherwise deemed worthy of prophecy makes an accurate prediction of the future three times in the presence of the Sanhedrin, then his prophecy is assumed to be true, and he is universally accepted as a prophet.[14] If, however, even the most minor aspect of his prophecy fails to come true, then his prophecy is judged to be completely false.[15] In the case of a false prophet, only the Sanhedrin has the authority to render judgment.[16]

Yad Avshalom, monument to Absalom, who attempted to depose his father, King David

Whenever a prophecy involved all Israel, it was pronounced before the Sanhedrin, since they were the only body that had the power to disseminate a message to the entire nation. Thus, for example, when Moses was sent by God with a message for

the Jewish people, he was first sent to the elders of the people, who convened a Sanhedrin to publicize his words.[17]

Apparently, the Sanhedrin kept a record of all prophecy that was meant for posterity. We thus find that the prophet Isaiah was killed before he was able to put his prophecies into writing; this was subsequently accomplished by the Sanhedrin under the leadership of King Hezekiah. Similarly, a number of the smaller prophetic books were written in their final form by the Sanhedrin led by Ezra the Scribe.[18]

The source of all prophetic inspiration was the Temple in Jerusalem, particularly the two Cherubim on the Ark of the Covenant that stood in the Holy of Holies.[19] In describing the Ark, God told Moses, "I will commune with you, and I

Opposite: *Excavations around Nebi Samwil, the burial site of the Prophet Samuel. At the* ***top*** *is a well;* ***below*** *are dwellings.*

Above: *Nebi Samuel, on a hill overlooking Jerusalem*

will speak with you from above the Ark-cover from between the two Cherubim, which are on the Ark of testimony" (Exodus 25:22).[20] What was true of Moses was also true of the other prophets, and the main influence of prophecy came through these two Cherubim in the Holy of Holies. There is some evidence that the prophetic experience actually came about through intense meditation on these two Cherubim.[21]

Each of the Cherubim had the form of a child with wings.[22] Although God had generally forbidden the construction of such images, He Himself had commanded that these two forms be placed over the Ark.[23] Rather than facing the people, the Cherubim faced each other. This clearly showed that they were not meant to be worshiped, but rather, that they indicated a place where spiritual force was concentrated.[24] The fact that the Cherubim stood on the Ark containing the Tablets and the original Torah scroll proves that these were the source of this spiritual power.

The fact that the Cherubim had the form of winged human beings means that man has the ability to transcend his earth-

Above: *Medieval era storefronts in the Cardo restoration, in the Old City*

Opposite: *The Tomb of King David*

ly bonds. Although man is bound to the earth by his mortal body, he can fly with the wings of his soul, soaring through the highest spiritual universes. This concept was embodied in the very shape of the Cherubim, and by meditating on them, a person could indeed fly with his own spiritual wings.

In order to explore this on a somewhat deeper level, we must look at the other important places where the Cherubim are mentioned in the Bible. After Adam and Eve were expelled from the Garden of Eden, the Torah states, "[God] expelled the man, and He placed the Cherubim at the east of the Garden of Eden ... to guard the way of the Tree of Life" (Genesis 3:24). The "Tree of Life" refers to the most profound spiritual experience; therefore, before one can enter into this experience, he must first encounter the Cherubim.[25] These Cherubim, of course, are a type of angel.

We then find the Cherubim in the vision of Ezekiel, which, according to the commentaries, is a paradigm of the prophetic experience in general.[26] The first thing that Ezekiel sees are the "Living Creatures" (*Chayot*), which are later identified as being the Cherubim.[27] The prophet reaches the highest levels of the mystical experience, actually transcending the bonds that tie his mind and soul to the physical world. In doing so, he is actually approaching the "Tree of Life," and the first thing that he encounters are its guardians, which are the Cherubim.

The Cherubim on the Ark were meant to parallel the Cherubim on high. Thus, in a sense, the space between these two forms was seen as an opening into the spiritual dimension.[28] In concentrating his thoughts between the Cherubim on the Ark, the prophet was able to pass between the angelic Cherubim, and ascend on the path of the Tree of Life. Conversely, when God's message was sent to the prophet, it followed this same path, first passing through the spiritual Cherubim, and then through those on the Ark. Hence, the space between the Cherubim was the source of all prophetic inspiration.[29]

Jerusalem was therefore the source of both Torah interpretation through the Sanhedrin and revelation through the

Street musicians entertain in a pedestrian mall in the City's center

prophets. It is thus written, "Out of Zion shall come forth the Torah, and the word of God from Jerusalem" (Isaiah 2:3, Micah 4:2). "Out of Zion shall come forth the Torah" refers primarily to the teachings of the Sanhedrin; since the name Zion is specific to the Hall of the Sanhedrin, "the gates marked (*zion*) by Law."[30] "The word of God from Jerusalem," on the other hand, refers to prophetic revelation.

The fact that the prophets and Sanhedrin worked hand in hand was very significant. In many religious societies, there is a strong conflict between the mystic and the teacher of religious law. There is always a danger that the mystic might consider himself above the law, or seek to change and modify it according to his own spiritual experiences. The prophets of Israel, however, were the greatest mystics that the world has ever seen, and yet, they clearly realized that the Torah was the very root of their power. The concept of mysticism and prophecy is included in the framework of the Torah law, and hence there could be no conflict. Furthermore, the prophets always worked very closely with the Sanhedrin; thus, they themselves were interpreters of the Law rather than its antagonists.

The Gate of Prayer

We enter "The Gate of Prayer" by going through the remains of the Hurva, once one of the Old City's principal synagogues

All the things we have discussed until now have been historical. The pilgrimages, the Temple, the Sanhedrin, kings and prophets no longer exist in Jerusalem, although, of course, their influence is strongly felt. But in many ways, Jerusalem is still considered a most important spiritual center for the Jew.

One area where Jerusalem still plays a most important role is that of prayer. All over the world, whenever a Jew stands in prayer, he faces Jerusalem. Every synagogue in the world is built with its ark on the side toward Jerusalem, so that all worshipers pray in that direction. Since both the United States and Europe are west of the Land of Israel, people in these countries always pray facing east.

The fact that prayer should be directed toward Jerusalem was indicated by King Solomon when he built the Temple. Upon dedicating the Temple, he prayed, "May You hearken to

Above: The Nissan Bok/Tiferes Yisrael Synagogue, another of the Old City's landmarks. As the pocked walls attest, it was a target of the Arab Legion in 1948.

Opposite: The Gates of Mercy in the Old City wall

the prayer of Your servant, and of Your people Israel, when they pray toward this place" (I Kings 8:30). Over and over in his dedication prayer, King Solomon stressed that prayers should be directed toward Jerusalem so that they would be accepted by God.[1] Later, when the Jews were exiled in Babylon, we find that Daniel faced Jerusalem in his three daily prayers.[2]

One reason for this is that Jacob called Jerusalem, "The gate of heaven" (Genesis 28:17). On a simple level, this means that it is the gate through which prayer ascends on high.[3] In a deeper sense, this also means that it is a gate through which one enters heaven by means of a mystical or prophetic experience, as discussed in the previous chapter. Regarding this it is also written, "This is the gate to God. Let the righteous enter into it" (Psalms 118:20).[4]

Jerusalem was only generally a focus of prayer; more specifically, it was the Holy Temple, and the place of the Ark in the Holy of Holies. A person standing in Jerusalem would face the Temple grounds, no matter where he was located. An individual praying in the Temple itself would face the Holy

The Rabban Yochanan ben Zakkai Synagogue, principal synagogue of the Sephardic community

Opposite: *Succos at the Kotel. Jews of all stripes join in reciting Hallel.*

of Holies, while a person actually praying in the Holy of Holies would face the Ark, directing himself to the point between the Cherubim.[5]

Here we begin to see a close parallel between prayer and prophecy. Just as the space between the Cherubim was the focus from which prophecy emanated, so it was the focus to which prayer was directed. To some degree, this can be understood in light of what Rabbi Jacob ben Asher writes in his *Tur,* that prayer itself is meant to be a highly mystical experience, where one can attain a level close to that of prophecy.[6] When a person stands in prayer, his mind ascends to the spiritual realm, and he can completely divorce himself from the physical. According to Rabbenu Yonah (Gerondi), this is the meaning of the teaching, "In prayer, one's eyes should be cast downward, while his heart is directed on high."[7]

Although this is a very high level of prayer, it is cited as being realizable in the *Shulchan Aruch*, the accepted Code of Jewish Law.[8] Therefore, when a person stands in prayer, he should attempt to direct his concentration toward the place of the Cherubim in the Holy of Holies, as the prophets did, because this is the path of spiritual ascent. Our sages thus teach us that

The joy of faith at the Kotel

Opposite: *Tallis, tefillin, machine gun, the Kotel — ingredients of life in Israel*

when a person prays, he should focus his mind on the Holy of Holies.[9] Of course, this does not mean that one's prayers should be directed to the Cherubim, or for that matter, anything else; all prayer must be directed only to God.[10]

Another reason we pray toward Jerusalem involves the close relationship between prayer and sacrifice. The prophet alluded to this relationship when he said, "We will make up for our bullocks with the offering of our lips" (Hosea 14:3).[11] It is thus established that the daily prayer services were ordained to take the place of the regular daily sacrifices.[12] Even today, in many ways, the laws involving prayer are derived from its relationship to the sacrifice, including the rule that it must be recited standing, with the feet together, and with one's head covered, just like a priest offering a sacrifice.[13] For the same reason, when standing in prayer, one must face Jerusalem, the place of sacrifice.[14]

In light of a number of concepts already discussed, it is

A relatively quiet moment at the Kotel — calm but always a magnet for prayer

***Opposite:** American young people on NCSY programs. The Kotel draws out the intensity, the holiness, the nucleus of the Jewish soul.*

easy to understand the relationship between prayer and sacrifice. The slaughtering and burning of the animal sacrifice symbolized the subjugation and destruction of the animal in man. When the animal was burned on the altar, it returned to its elements and ascended on high. When a person brought a sacrifice, he was able to meditate on this, nullifying his animal self, and liberating his spirit so that it could commune with God. The soul then returned to its own element, which is the spiritual. Therefore, the bringing of a sacrifice was a highly mystical experience. The Hebrew word for sacrifice, *Korban,* comes from the root *Karav,* meaning "close," since it brought man close to God.[15]

The concept of prayer is very similar to this. When a person stands before God, he becomes a total spiritual being, totally divorced from his animal self. The only difference is that instead of experiencing this through sacrifice, the individual does so through uttering words of prayer.

The final reason we pray toward Jerusalem is that it was

the place of the Sanhedrin, and as such, it was the chief location of schools where the Torah was taught. Thus, when we focus our prayers toward Jerusalem, we are also combining them with the merit of the Torah, through which they become more acceptable before God.[16] As mentioned earlier, even when worship services were held in the Temple itself, they were held in the Hall of the Sanhedrin.

Looking through the prayer book, one readily sees that virtually every major part of the service contains some mention of Jerusalem.[17] Besides the fact that we must physically face Jerusalem, it appears that there must also be a mention of Jerusalem in every prayer, whereby the prayer is bound to the Holy City. By mentioning Jerusalem in prayer, we actually help focus the prayer through the "Gate of Heaven."

Even though the Altar, the Cherubim, and the Sanhedrin no longer stand in Jerusalem, the place retains its special holiness. The holiness of Jerusalem pertains to God's presence, which can never be nullified.[18] For this reason, even today, it is forbidden to enter the place where the Temple originally stood.[19] But in a positive sense, because of its unique history and sig-

Yeshivah Bircas HaTorah in the Eitz Chaim building of the Old City, attracting adults in quest of their heritage

nificance, Jerusalem is still the focal point of all our prayers.

The fact that Jerusalem is the "Gate of Heaven" has another important implication. Just as things can go in through a gate, so can they emerge. Thus, all spiritual sustenance and blessing come only through Jerusalem, as it is written, "God will bless you from Zion" (Psalms 128:5).[20] It is taught that God first sends a blessing to Jerusalem, and from there it flows to the entire world.[21] Today, when the Temple no longer stands, the source of this blessing is the Western Wall.[22]

Afterword

by Rabbi Baruch Taub

Rabbi Nachman said, "Wherever I go, I go to Jerusalem." And so it is for every Jew. The eternal message of Jerusalem accompanies the Jew every day of his life. He longs for Jerusalem, the "city of peace," to find its complete fulfillment. He mourns for its Temple, temporarily removed from its people.

Daily we pray for Jerusalem, "the mother of Israel." She is brought to mind when we thank G-d for our food, in our Sabbath and holy-day observances, and in our prayers. Even when we paint and plaster our homes we leave an empty space to recall Jerusalem.

Under the bridal canopy, ashes are placed upon the head of the bridegroom and a glass is broken in solemn remembrance of Jerusalem. When a Jew dies, earth of Jerusalem is placed inside the coffin.

The entire Jewish people concludes the Passover seder and the Yom Kippur service with a unified insistence that the end of our longing for her comfort is nigh by proclaiming: "Next year in Jerusalem."

We are in love with Jerusalem. It is this love which causes us to call upon her at every opportunity. We cannot remove her from our thoughts. As the Talmud relates: "Ten measures of beauty descended to this world. Nine were given to Jerusalem and one to the rest of the world."

Clearly, in the Jewish experience, Jerusalem is everywhere. More than a city, Jerusalem is a basic Jewish concept which affects the heart of Jewish life in every age.

The events of 28 Iyar 5727 (June 7, 1967) which mark the reunification of Jerusalem under Jewish rule were historic for Jews all over the world. Jerusalem, the capital of Israel, is a great modern-day occurrence.

It is the purpose of this book, however, to go beyond the geography, inhabitants, history and capital that is Jerusalem. The primary goal of this work is to explain why Jerusalem has preoccupied the Jewish conscience through every period of Jewish history, to define Jerusalem the religious concept rather than Jerusalem the city.

Bearing this in mind, it would be unfair to conclude that omissions were made in this treatment of Jerusalem. "Jerusalem: Eye of the Universe" is a thorough and exhaustive study of a major tenet of our Torah.

Once again we are grateful to the noted scholar, Rabbi Aryeh Kaplan, for gracing the NCSY library of publications with another masterful presentation.

Ramban (*Nachmanides*) stated in 1268: "The glory of the world is Eretz Yisroel; the glory of Eretz Yisroel is Jerusalem; the glory of Jerusalem is the Holy Temple."

May the glory of the *Shechinah* be restored to the rebuilt Temple speedily, in our day.

"*Leshana Haba B'Yerushalayim*"; Next Year in Jerusalem!

Notes

INTRODUCTION

1. *Orach Chaim* 560:2, *Even HaEzer* 65:3 in *Hagah*.
   See *Tosafot, Berakhot* 31a, s.v. "*Isi.*"

BEGINNINGS

1. Deuteronomy 12:5, 11, 14, 18, 21, 26; 14:23, 24, 25; 15:20; 16:2, 7, 15, 17, 17:8, 10, 15; 26:2; 31:11.
2. *Moreh Nebukhim* 3:45, Bachya on Deuteronomy 12:5. See Radak on 1 Kings 8:16.
3. See *Zohar* 2:198a, Abarbanel, *Kli Yakar*, on Deuteronomy 12:5.
4. *Yerushalmi, Nazir* 7:2, *Targum J.*, Rashi, on Genesis 2:7, *Bereshit Rabbah* 14:8, *Midrash Tehillim* 92:6, *Tanchuma, Pekudey* 3, *Pirkey Rabbi Eliezer* 12, 20, *Tana DeBei Eliahu Zuta* 2, Bachya on Deuteronomy 32:43. Also see *Sanhedrin* 38b (top).
5. *Yad, Bet HaBechirah* 2:2.
6. *Tosefta, Chulin* 3:7, *Shabbat* 28b, *Chulin* 60a, from Psalms 69:32. According to one tradition, this was offered on the first Sunday after Adam was created, see *Avodah Zarah 8a, Etz Yosef, Rif* (Pinto) *ad loc.* (in Eyin *Yaakov*), *Avot Rav Natan 1:6, Targum J.* to Genesis 8:20. There are some opinions that Adam was not driven out of the Garden of Eden until Saturday night, since the merit of the Sabbath protected him, see *Pirkey Rabbi Eliezer* 19 (44a), *Kuzari* 2:20 (26a), *Kol Yehudah ad loc.* According to another tradition, however, he was driven out on a Friday afternoon, see *Sanhedrin* 38b, *Yalkut* (758) on Psalms 49:21. Also see *Pirkey Rabbi Eliezer* 20, *Shaar HaGamul* (in *Kitvey Ramban*) p. 296. *Cf.* Ramban on Genesis 2:8, *Bereshit Rabbah* 16:5.
7. *Targum J.* on Genesis 22:9.
8. *Pirkey Rabbi Eliezer* 20 (47b). This also took place on Sunday morning.
9. *Targum J.* on Genesis 8:30, *Pirkey Rabbi Eliezer* 31 (70b), *Yad, loc. cit.*, Rekanti on Genesis 8:20.
10. *Targum J.* on Genesis 8:20, 22:19, *Bereshit Rabbah* 34:9. This might be related to the question as to whether the flood destroyed the Land of Israel, see *Zevachim* 113b.
11. *VaYikra Rabbah* 20:1, *Tanchuma, Noah 9.* Shem was not the oldest son, but the foremost in wisdom and piety; *Sanhedrin* 69b, *Bereshit Rabbah* 26:3, Rashi on Genesis 5:32.
12. *Cf.* Isaiah 54:9.
13. See Rashi, *Midrash Agadah, Chizkuni*, on Genesis 12:6.
14. *Bereshit Rabbah* 56:10, *Midrash Tehillim* 76:3.
15. See notes 21, 34, 37, 39, 43, 55, 56.
16. Genesis 14:18, Rashi, *Targum J. ad loc.*; Psalms 110:4; Radak, Ralbag, on Joshua 10:1; *Nedarim* 32b.
17. *Bereshit Rabbah* 43:6, Ibn Ezra, Ramban, Hirsch, on Genesis 14:18. *Cf.* Isaiah 1:26.
18. See *Midrash Pinchas ben Yair* (*Midrash Tadsheh*) 22, in *Bet HaMidrash* 3:192, *Otzar Midrashim* 2:474; Abarbanel on Joshua 15:63, Judges 1:21, 19:12, 2 Samuel 5:6. *Cf.* Josephus, *Antiquities* 7:3:1, 5:2:2. Also see Arkhin 32b, that there were two cities called Jerusalem.
19. This explains why God told Abraham to go to the Land of Moriah (Genesis 21:2), while Malchi-tzedek was said to be the king of Salem. See Moreh *Nebukhim* 3:45. This may be related to the discussion regarding the meaning of the name Moriah. If Moriah also indicates teaching (*Horah*), then it also includes the place of the Sanhedrin. See Chapter 3, note 33.
20. Noah's Altar was destroyed in the Generation of Separation after the building of the Tower of Babel, *Targum J.* on Genesis 22:9, Radal on *Pirkey Rabbi Eliezer* 31:33. After that, Moriah was in Amorite territory, see Rashbam, *Chizkuni*, on Genesis 22:2. Also see Ramban, end of commentary on Genesis 10:16. Regarding this conquest, see note 13. There is, however, a tradition that the builders were wiped away by a tidal wave, see *Bereshit Rabbah* 38:11.
21. *Sefer HaYashar* (Ed. Alter Bergman, Tel Aviv) p. 23. This is disputed by the tradition that Abraham had no teacher, see *Bereshit Rabbah* 61:1.
22. *Zohar* 1:78a, Rashi on Genesis 12:9; *Bereshit Rabbah* 39:16, Radak on Genesis 12:9.
23. *Nedarim* 32b, Ran *ad loc.* "*U'Malchi-tzedek,*" *Pirkey Rabbi Eliezer* 8 (18b). Radal *ad loc.* 8:17; *Bereshit Rabbah* 43:6.
24. Genesis 21:23; Rashi on Joshua 15:63, quoting *Sifri* on Deuteronomy12:17. (In our editions of *Sifri*, this statement regarding the oath is lacking, and Rashi there speaks of a different oath, see note 33.) Also see Rashi, Radak, on 2 Samuel 5:6, *Siftey Chachamim* on Deuteronomy 12:17. This was besides the oath that Abraham later made with Ephron, see *Tosafot Shantz, Sotah* 10a, Maharitz Chajot *ad loc.* Also see *Bereshit Rabbah* 54:2, *Mekhilta* on Exodus 13:17.
25. See commentaries on *Avot* 5:3.
26. *Bereshit Rabbah* 56:1, *VaYikra Rabbah* 20:2, *Kohelet Rabbah* 9:2, *Tanchuma, VaYer* 23.
27. *Pirkey Rabbi Eliezer* 31, Radal *ad loc.* 31:9, 28.
28. *Pesikta Rabatai* 40, *Yalkut* 2:988. See *Bereshit Rabbah 55:7, Nedarim* 32b.
29. Genesis 22:14, Rosh *ad loc.*
30. *Baaley Tosafot* on Genesis 22:14, *Midrash Tehillim* 76:3, *Bereshit Rabbah* 56:10; *Tosafot, Taanit* 16a, s.v. *"Har," Minchat Shai* on Joshua 10:5. From the general context, it appears that Moriah or Jeru was the western half of the city, while Salem was to the east. See *Midrash Pinchas ben Yair, loc. cit.*, that David united these two parts of the city to form Jerusalem.
31. See *Berakhot* 62b, *Zevachim* 62a, *Kuzari* 2:14 (17a) Josephus, *Antiquities* 7:13:4.
32. In Joshua 15:9, there is a mention of Mount Ephron near Jerusalem. (This might be the present Mt. Zion.) Abraham lived at peace with at least some of the Amorites, see Genesis 14:13. *Cf.* Genesis 15:16.
33. *Pirkey Rabbi Eliezer* 36 (84b), *Midrash HaGadol* on Genesis 23:13, Rashi on Deuteronomy 12:17, Radak on *2* Samuel 5:6, *Tosafot Shantz loc. cit.* See *Mekhilta* on Exodus 13:11, Malbim (18), *Meir Eyin, ad loc.* See note 24.
34. *Bereshit Rabbah* 56:11. Isaac did not return with Abraham, Genesis 22:19, *Targum J. ad loc.* When Abraham took Isaac to Mount Moriah, he told Sarah that he was bringing him to Shem's academy, *Tanchuma, VaYera* 22, *Midrash HaGadol* on Genesis 22:3, *Sefer HaYashar* pp. 59, 60. Isaac mourned Sarah for three years before marrying Rebecca, *Pirkey Rabbi Eliezer* 32 (73a). Also see *Yoma* 28b.
35. *Pesachim* 88a, Rashi *ad loc. s.v. "Har," Tosafot, Berakhot* 34b, s.v. "*Chatzif.*" Isaac instituted the afternoon service, *Berakhot* 26b, *Yad, Melakhim 9:1.* It was called a field since it was not inhabited.
36. *Targum J.* on Genesis 25:21, *Pirkey Rabbi Eliezer* 32 (73a). *Cf. Zohar* 1:137a. Some say that Rebecca was with him when he offered this prayer, see *Bereshit Rabbah* 63:5, Rashi on Genesis 25:21.

37. *Targum J.* on Genesis 25:22, *Bereshit Rabbah* 63:6, *Pirkey Rabbi Eliezer* 32, Radal *ad loc.* 32:29. We find that Rebecca prayed on Mt. Moriah, see *Sefer HaYashar* p. 69. Also see Rashi, Ramban, on Genesis 25:22, *Moreh Nebukhim* 2:41 (end).
38. Rashbam on Genesis 25:28, Ramban on Genesis 27:4, Zohar 1:139a.
39. *Targum J.*, Rashi, on Genesis 25:27, *Bereshit Rabbah* 63:10, *Tanchuma B, VaYishlach 9.* Until this time, it appears that Shem and Eber shared the same academy. This is the first mention that Eber had his own school. However, the reason why they are spoken of separately may be because Jacob studied in Eber's academy after the death of Shem.
40. *Bava Batra* 16b, *Bereshit Rabbah* 63:11. Jacob was 15 years old when Abraham died, since Abraham lived to be 175 years old, Abraham was 100 when Isaac was born, and Isaac was 60 years old when Jacob was born. See *Sedar HaDorot* 2123. Regarding the sale, see *Tshuvot HaRivash* 328.
41. *Targum J.* on Genesis 27:27, *Bereshit Rabbah* 65:23, *Tanchuma B, Toldot* 10, *Agadat Bereshit* 42, *Sifri* on Deuteronomy 33:12.
42. *Bereshit Rabbah* 66:3, *Tanchuma B, Toldot* 16.
43. *Megillah* 17a, Rashi on Genesis 25:17, 28:9.
44. *Pesachim* 88a, *Targum*, Rashi, Ramban, on Genesis 28:11, *Targum* on 2 Chronicles 3:1, 21:15, *Pirkey Rabbi Eliezer* 35, *Bereshit Rabbah* 69:7, *Kuzari* 2:14 (f7a). Even though the Torah states that this "House of God" was originally called Luz (Genesis 28:19), this might have been a name for the point in Jerusalem where creation began, see Bachya, *Tzioni, ad loc.*, *Bereshit Rabbah* 69:8, Radak, HaGra, on Joshua 16:1, Rashi on Joshua 18:13, Judges 1:23, 26. God saw the merit of Jacob in this place, *Berakhot* 62b. Jacob initiated the evening service, *Berakhot* 26b, *Yad, Melakhim 9:1.*
45. *Pirkey Rabbi Eliezer* 35, *Midrash Tehillim* 91:7, *Zohar* 1:131a, 1:72a. Some say that he slept in Beer Sheva, Bachya on Genesis 28:18. Also see Bachya on Genesis 28:10, *Bereshit Rabbah* 68:5, Radal (3, 4), Maharzav, *ad loc.*, Radak on Psalms 132:2.
46. According to some authorities, the verse, "Jacob came to Salem, a city of Shechem" (Genesis 33:18), is to be interpreted to mean that he actually returned to Jerusalem at this time. See *Maaseh HaShem*, Rashbam, *ad loc.*, *Zohar* 1:172b, Bachya on Deuteronomy 21:9. Another opinion is that it was a different Salem in the territory of Shechem, Abarbanel *ad loc.* Others write that the city called Shechem was in the land of Salem, *Sefer HaYashar*, p. 87. This position is supported by the fact that every place in the Bible where the word *Shalem* appears meaning "perfect," it is in conjunction with the word "heart," indicating a "perfect heart." The only exception is 2 Chronicles 8:18, but there *Shalem* can also be interpreted to be a place name. Others, however, maintain that in the short verse, *Shalem* means "complete," so that the verse reads, "Jacob came complete to the city of Shechem." See Rashi, *Midrash Lekach Tov, Chizkuni*, Ibn Ezra, *Targum, ad loc.*, *Shabbat* 33b.We find (Genesis 33:19) that Jacob bought a parcel of a field in this area, and in Joshua 24:32 we see that this parcel is actually in the city of Shechem, this being the place where Joseph is buried. There are firm traditions that Joseph is buried in Shechem and not in Jerusalem.
47. Genesis 33:7. See *Torah Temimah*, Genesis 32:9, Deuteronomy 33:45. At this time, however, Rachel was already pregnant with Benjamin, see *Targum J.* on Genesis 32:25. *Pirkey Rabbi Eliezer* 37 (87a). See *Esther Rabbah* 7:8.
48. See Genesis 32:25, Alshich *ad loc.* See my pamphlet, "The Jew," Collegiate Hashkafa Series, Young Israel, New York, 1973, pp. 5, 6.
49. Genesis 35:1, 7, 15, *Midrash Lekach Tov ad loc.*, *Bereshit Rabbah* 78:16, Radal, Maharzav *ad loc.*
50. *Sifri* on Deuteronomy 33:12. Benjamin was born in the year 2208, while Reuben was born in 2193, Judah in 2195, and Joseph in 2199. See *Seder HaDorot.*
51. *Sotah* 37a, *Tosefta, Berakhot* 4:16, *Mekhilta* on Exodus 14:23, *Zohar* 2:158b. Also see *Zohar* 1:89a, that Judah was given dominion because his name is identical to the Tetragrammaton, except for the *Dalet*, which stands for David. Regarding Simon and Levi, see *Targum J.*, Rashi, *Midrash HaGadol, Midrash Lekach Tov*, on Genesis 49:6.
52. *Bereshit Rabbah* 99:1. It was not in Joseph's portion, since the other brothers were punished because of him, Radal *ad loc.* 99:3. Joseph was sold at the age of 17 in the year 2216, and Benjamin was eight years old at the time.
53. Genesis 38:29, 46:12, Ruth 4:18-22. This took place in the year 2228. Judah's rule was enhanced at this time, see *Sotah* 37a, *Tosefta, Berakhot* 4:16.
54. *Sanhedrin* 56b, Tosefta, *Avodah Zarah* 9:4, *Yad, Melakhim 9:1.*
55. *Bereshit Rabbah* 67:8.
56. *Yerushalmi, Sanhedrin* 4:7 (22b), *Karban HaEdah ad loc.* (4:8), *Tanchuma B, VaYeshev* 17, *Esther Rabbah* 4:6, *Yafeh Nof ad loc.* It was also in this court that a decree was issued against premarital intercourse, see *Avodah Zarah* 36b.
57. Genesis 43:8, 44:14, 44:18, *Bereshit Rabbah* 84:17. Judah was sent by Jacob to establish an academy in Egypt, see *Targum J.*, Rashi, on Genesis 46:28, *Bereshit Rabbah* 95:3, *Tanchuma, VaYigash* 11.
58. *Targum J.*, Rashi, *ad loc.*, *Megillah* 16b. See Psalms 78:67, and also see note 52.
59. Rashi *ad loc.*, *Bereshit Rabbah* 98:8, *Sifri* on Deuteronomy 33:12, *Rashi, Zevachim* 54b, s.v. *"Velka."*
60. *Targum*, Rashi, *Midrash Agadah, ad loc.*, Rashi on Deuteronomy 12:14, Rashi, *Zevachim* 53b *"Toref,"* Bertenoro, *Middot* 3:1 (end), *Zevachim* 5:4.
61. *Zevachim* 53b.
62. *Zevachim* 55b, *Tosafot Yeshenim, Yoma* 12a.
63. *Seder Olam Rabbah* 3, *Seder HaDorot* 2331, *Midrash Pinchas ben Yair* (*Midrash Tadsheh*) 8, Bachya on Exodus 1:6. See *BaMidbar Rabbah* 13:8, *Targum J.* on Exodus 6:16, *Shir HaShirim Rabbah* 4:7. Levi had already been chosen by Jacob as the "tithe" of his twelve children, see *Pirkey Rabbi Eliezer* 37 (87a).
64. *Sotah* 12a, Maharitz Chajot *ad loc.*, *Shemot Rabbah* 1:13, 19, *Shir HaShirim Rabbah* 2:8, *Kohelet Rabbah* 9:17, *Yad, Melakhim 9:1, Tshuvot Makom Shmuel* 23.
65. *Tanchuma B, VaArah* 4, *BaHaAlotecha* 13; *Yad, Avodat Kokhavim* 1:3, *Issury Biah* 13:2.
66. *Mekhilta* on Exodus 14:22.
67. *Sifri* on Numbers 9:5, *Sifri, Targum J.*, Rashi, on Deuteronomy 33:8-10, *Midrash Tehillim* 1:14.
68. Rashi on Deuteronomy 33:12.
69. *Yoma* 12a, *Megillah* 26a, *Zevachim* 53b, 118b.
70. Mountains refer to Jerusalem, see note 73.
71. *Pirkey Rabbi Eliezer* 36 (84b), Rashi, Radak, on Joshua 15:63.
72. *Mekhilta* on Exodus 13:11. See *VaYikra Rabbah* 17:6, *Devarim Rabbah* 5:14, *Yerushalmi, Shevi'it* 6:1 (16a). See *Sanhedrin* 91a, with regard to their complaint to Alexander the Great, that there were African tribes who were descendants of the Canaanites. The Hittites, Jebusites and Amorites were all descendants of Zidon, Genesis 10:16. The Jebusite was one of the tribes promised to Abraham, Genesis 15:21. Also see Ezra 9:1.
73. *Sifri*, Rashi, Hirsch, *ad loc.*
74. See Chapter 7, note 20.

DEDICATION

1. *Sifri* on Numbers 10:32, Deuteronomy 12:5, 33:12, Rashi on Numbers 10:32, *Tosafot, Bava Kama* 82b, s.v. *"VeAin."*
2. *Siyach Yitzchak* on *Yoma* 12a, *Petach Eynayim* (Chidah) on *Zevachim* 54b. See *Megillah* 26a, *Yad, Tumat Tzaraat* 14:11, *Bet HaBechirah* 7:14, Ralbag on Joshua 12:5. Cf. 1 Kings 11:32, *Tosafot Yom Tov* on *Negaim* 12:4, *Zevachim* 5:4. All tribes are partners in Jerusalem, *Avot Rav Natan* 35:3, Rashi on Deuteronomy 12:14. From Rambam on *Negaim* 12:4 (end), however, there seems to be an indication that Jerusalem may actually be an international city, since he derives it from Isaiah 56:7, "My house is a house of prayer for all peoples." See *Minchat Chinuch* 177:4, that the ground was divided but not the airspace, *cf. Zevachim* 54a.
3. Joshua 10:3, 5, 12:10.
4. Joshua 10:12-14.
5. Joshua 10:5. See Chapter 6, note 18.
6. *Shalshelet HaKabalah* (Jerusalem 5722) p. 225, *Seder HaDorot* 2478.
7. *Pa'at HaShulchan* 3:14, *Bet Yisrael ad loc.* 3:33. See *Arkhin* 9:6 (32a).
8. Ralbag on Judges 19:10, Abarbanel on Judges 1:8, Radal on *Pirkey Rabbi Eliezer* 36:78; *Midrash Pinchas ben Yair*, quoted above in Chapter 6, note 18. Others, however, maintain that Joshua himself conquered Jerusalem.
9. See *Bava Batra* 118a, b, Rashi on Numbers 26:54, HaGra on Joshua 17:14.
10. See Malbim, HaGra, on Joshua 15:8, Radak on Joshua 18:28.
11. *Yoma* 12a, *Megillah* 26a.
12. *Rashi ad loc.* See Chapter 6, note 24.
13. See Chapter 6, note 18.
14. Regarding the question when the episode of the concubine in Givah occurred, see *Seder HaDorot* 2516, 2764, 2811.
15. See Rashi *ad loc.*, Rashi, *Sanhedrin* 44b, s.v. *"Avikha Emori."*
16. *Sotah* 10a, *Tosafot Shantz ad loc.* David did not yet know that Jerusalem was the chosen city, see Ibn Ezra on Psalms 51:20, Rashi, *Makkot* lla, s.v. *"Nasa."* Until Psalm 51, there is no mention of Jerusalem at all. In Judges

17:57, we find that David also brought Goliath's head to Saul, while in Josephus, *Antiquities* 6:9:5, we find that he brought it to his own house. See Malbim on Judges 17:57. This may be a hint to the tradition that the Philistines had lived in Jerusalem and were protected by a covenant.

17. *Sifri*, Ramban, on Deuteronomy 12:5. It may be that the city must be ascertained logically, while the place of the Altar is to be revealed by a prophet.
18. *Ibid.*, Abarbanel on 2 Samuel 24:24. See Rashi, *Makkot* 11a, s.v. *"Nasa."*
19. Radak on Psalms 132:2.
20. *Zevachim* 55b, *Sifri* on Deuteronomy 33:12, Rashi, *Makkot loc. cit.* See 1 Kings 8:16.
21. *Ibid.* Another sign was the fact that Jerusalem was the only city divided between two tribes, see *Tosafot Yeshenim, Yoma* 12a, s.v. *"Ma Haya," Sanhedrin* 111a.
22. *Sanhedrin* 20a, Rashi, *Tosafot, ad loc.* s.v. *"Shtey," Tzemach David* 2892, *Seder HaDorot* 2889; Radak on 2 Samuel 5:3, 1 Chronicles 11:4.
23. See Chapter 6, note 18. *Cf.* Rashi, Radak, Abarbanel, on 2 Samuel 5:6, *Pirkey Rabbi Eliezer* 36. See *Midrash Tehillim* 18:24.
24. *Midrash Pinchas ben Yair*, quoted in Chapter 6, note 18.
25. There is considerable evidence that the Jews lived in peace with the Hittites, see Radak on 2 Samuel 11:3, *Kiddushin* 76b. Also see Judges 1:26, 1 Samuel 26:6, 1 Kings 10:29, 11:1, 2 Kings 7:6, 1 Chronicles 11:41.
26. 2 Samuel 5:17, 1 Chronicles 11:3, Rashi on 1 Chronicles 14:8. This valley was to the south of Jerusalem, see Joshua 15:8. The *Metzudah* is identified with *Metzudot Tzion*, and it was on the eastern side of the mountain. Psalms 2 was said at this time, see Radak on Psalms 2:1, 2 Samuel 5:17.
27. See Radak *ad loc.*, 1 Chronicles 16:1. Psalms 105 was said at this time, see Ibn Ezra, Radak, on Psalms 105:1, and also see 1 Chronicles 16:8. See *Bet Yosef* on *Tur, Orach Chaim* 50, s.v. *"BiZman."*
28. 1 Chronicles 16:39, 22:29, 1 Kings 3:4. See Chapter 2, note 6.
29. 2 Samuel 8:7, Rashi, Radak, *ad loc.*
30. Rashi on Deuteronomy 12:10.
31. Also 1 Chronicles 17:1.
32. Radak *ad loc.* See 1 Kings 5:17, 1 Chronicles 28:3, Abarbanel on 2 Samuel 7:13.
33. 2 Samuel 24, 1 Chronicles 21. See *Zohar* 2:125b, Ramban, *Or HaChaim, Paneach Raza*, on *Exodus* 30:12, Radak on 1 Samuel 15:4, 2 Samuel 24:1, *Midrash Tehillim* 17:4. See note 31.
34. *Yad, Bet HaBechirah* 2:1, *Targum* on 1 Chronicles 21:15, 2 Chronicles 3:1. See *Zevachim* 62a.
35. *Midrash Shmuel* 30, *Pesikta* 11 (43a), Radak on Psalms 51:16. There are only two places where David says, "I have sinned before God," one being here, 2 Samuel 24:10, and the other being with regard to Bathsheba and Uriah, 2 Samuel 12:13. In *Berakhot* 62b, we find that David was tempted to count Israel because he called God a Tempter (1 Samuel 26:9, see Radak *ad loc.*) with regard to Saul. Thus, there are two places where the Scripture says of David, "His heart smote him," here (2 Samuel 24:10)and with regard to Saul (1 Samuel 24:16). It might be that because he called God a Tempter that he was tempted with Bathsheba, and this entire episode then was decreed to happen.
36. 1 Samuel 11, 12.
37. *Avodah Zarah* 4b. See *Shabbat* 55b that whoever says that David sinned is mistaken.
38. *Yerushalmi, Peah* 1:1 (5a), *Sanhedrin* 10:1 (49a), *Zohar* 2:106a, *Emunot VeDeyot* 5:6, *Yad, Tshuvah* 3:14.
39. It is significant to note that Psalms 51 was said with regard to Bathsheba; Psalms 51:20 is the first mention of Jerusalem as a place of sacrifice, and indeed, the very first mention of Jerusalem in the *Book of Psalms*. It is thus evident that the episode involving Bathsheba is closely related to the revelation of the chosen place to David.
40. Rashi, Bachya, *Chizkuni, ad loc., Berakhot* 62b, *Tanchuma, Ki Tisa 9, Pesikta* 2 (18b), *Zohar* 2:125b. It is important to note that the half-shekel was intended as an atonement for the Golden Calf. It is taught in *Avodah Zarah* 4b that the main purpose of the episode involving the Golden Calf was also to teach the power of repentance. Regarding the relationship of the half-shekel and the Golden Calf, see *Yerushalmi, Shekalim* 2:3, *Midrash HaGadol* on Exodus 30:11.
41. Exodus 38:26, 27; Rashi on Exodus 30:15.
42. *Sifri* on Deuteronomy 12:5.
43. 2 Samuel 24:25, 1 Chronicles 21:25; Abarbanel on 2 Samuel 24:25, *Zevachim* 116b, *Pirkey Rabbi Eliezer* 36 (85b), *Sifri* on Numbers 6:26, Deuteronomy 12:6, Rashi, *Yoma* 12a *"Eleh,"* Rashi on Deuteronomy 12:14, *Tosafot, Ketubot* 99a, s.v. *"Natan," Bekhorot* 50a, s.v. *"DeMizdavana."*
44. 1 Chronicles 22:2 *ff.*, 29:2 *ff.*
45. *Succah* 53a, Rashi, *Makkot* 11a, s.v. *"SheKara,"* Maharsha, *Succah* 49a, 53a. Rashi writes that David dug these foundations even before he bought the place from Arnon.
46. *Yerushalmi, Sanhedrin* 10:2 (52b), *Megillah* 1:1 (1b). See 1 Chronicles 27:33, Rashi, Radak, on 1 Chronicles 28:19. This was based on a scroll handed down from the time of Moses, see *Midrash Shmuel* 15 (end), *Agadat Bereshit* 37. Others, however, state that it was revealed to the prophets Nathan and Gad, see Rashi, *Succah* 51b, s.v. *"HaKall."* See Rashi, *Eruvin* 104a, s.v. *"Ka Mosif."* Also see *Iggeret Moshe, Orach Chaim* 39.
47. *Eruvin* 104a, *Pesachim* 86a, *Succah* 51b, *Zevachim* 33a, 62a, *Chulin* 83b, *Bekhorot* 17b.
48. 1 Kings 1:38, 39.
49. 1 Kings 3:1, Abarbanel *ad loc.* There were three walls around Jerusalem, see 1 Kings 9:15, 19, Josephus, *Antiquities* 8:2:1, 8:6:1. There is also a mention of building the walls of Jerusalem in Psalms 51:20.
50. See *Pesachim* 54a, *Bereshit Rabbah* 1:4.
51. See *Targum*, Ralbag *ad loc., Kuzari* 2:14 (17a). Also see Josephus, *Antiquities* 7:13:4, 7:3, 8:2.
52. *Zevachim* 62a. As before, the place of the Altar had to be revealed through a prophet, see note 17.
53. According to traditional Jewish chronology, the second Temple stood for 420 years, see *Seder Olam Rabbah* 28, *Yoma* 9a, *Yerushalmi, Yoma* 1:1, *Tosefta, Zevachim* 13:3, Rashi, *Avodah Zarah* 9a, s.v. *"Ki Mayanta."* According to this tradition, the second Temple was built in 350 B.C.E., while according to secular historians it was built in 516 B.C.E., or 166 years earlier. Josephus also has a different chronology, see *Antiquities* 20:10, *Wars* 6:10. For a discussion of this, see *Tzemach David* 2:3842, *Seder HaDorot* 3828. The 420 years include 34 of Persian rule, 180 of Greece, 103 of the Hasmonians, and 103 of Herod. See commentaries on Daniel 9:25, *Seder HaKabalah* (Abraham ben Daud) p. 6.
54. *Taanit* 4:6 (26a).
55. See Chapter 5, note 19.
56. *Bava Batra* 60b, *Tosefta, Sotah* 15:12-14, *Orach Chaim* 560: 1.
57. *Moed Katan* 26a, *Tosefta, Nedarim* 1:4, *Orach Chaim* 561.
58. *Yalkut* 2:1009.
59. *Taanit* 30b.

REBIRTH

1. *Sanhedrin 98a, Or HaChaim* on Numbers 24:17; *Emunot VeDeyot* 8:5, 6. See *The Real Messiah* (NCSY, New York, 1973) p. 65.
2. *Sanhedrin* 98a, Maharsha *ad loc. "Ad SheTikhla."*
3. Ramban on Song of Songs 8:12, Radak on Psalms 146:3, *Derishat Tzion* 1:2 (p. 90).
4. *Sanhedrin* 98a.
5. *Tshuvot Chatam Sofer, Yoreh Deah* 234, *Petach HaDevir* 3:319d, *Din Emet* (Responsa at end of volume) 2, *Mateh Aaron* 2:274c, *Pitchey Tshuvah, Yoreh Deah* 251:4. Also see *Tshuvot Chatam Sofer, Orach Chaim* 203.
6. *Berakhot* 49a, *Tanchuma, Noah* 11. Also see *Midrash* quoted in *Sheveiley Emunah* 10:1 (93d), *Megillah* 17b, Maharsha *ad loc.*
7. *Iggeret Teimon p.* 30. See Joel 3:1, 5.
8. Radak *ad loc., Eruvin* 43b, *Eduyot* 8:7, *Targum J.* on Deuteronomy 39:4, *Pirkey Rabbi Eliezer* 43. Also see *Yad, Melakhim* 10:2, *Kereiti U'Peleiti*, end of *Bet HaSafek*.
9. *Yad, Melakhim* 1:3. See Chapter 4, note 1.
10. *Yad, Tshuvah* 9:2. See *Targum*, Abarbanel on Isaiah 11:2, Mahari Kara, *Kli Paz*, on Isaiah 52:13; *Tanchuma, Toledot* 14, *Agadat Bereshit* 45. "Coming of the Messiah" is the time when the Messiah attains this spirit of prophecy and realizes his mission, see *Arba Meot Shekel Kesef* (Cracow, 5646) p. 68c.
11. *Mekhilta* on Exodus 12:1, *Tanchuma, Bo* 5; Rashi, Radak, on Jonah 1:3, *Zohar* I:85a, 1:12la, 2:170b, *Emunot VeDeyot* 3:5, *Kuzari* 2:14, Ibn Ezra on Joel 3:1, *Tshuvot Radbaz* 2:842. The only one who apparently disputes this is Abraham Abulafia, see *Sefer HaCheshek* (*Ms.* JTS 1801)p. 32a *ff.*
12. *Yoma* 9b, *Kuzari* 2:24 (40a).
13. *Sifri*, Ramban, on Deuteronomy 18:15.
14. Thus, if the generation is not worthy of prophecy, it cannot exist, even though there might be worthy individuals. See *Sanhedrin* 11a, *Berakhot* 57a, *Succah* 28a, *Bava Batra* 134a; *Tosefta, Sotah* 13:4. *Pirkey Rabbi Eliezer* 8 (20b), *Avot Rabbi Natan* 14:1. Also see *Taanit* 30b, *Bava Batra* 121a (end), *Tosafot ad loc.* s.v. *"Yom," Mekhilta* to Exodus 12:1, *Sifra* on Leviticus 1:1; *Yerushalmi, Taanit* 3:4 (15a), *Shir HaShirim Rabbah* 2:27, Rashi on Deuteronomy 2:16.
15. *Yad, Melakhim* 11:4. See *Yerushalmi, Maaser Sheni* 5:2 (*29b*), *Tosafot Yom Tov*, Rashash,

Malechet Shlomo ad loc., Shnei Luchot HaBrit, Bet David 1:37b, *Petil Tekhelet* (in *Shloshet Sifrey Tekhelet,* Jerusalem, 5723) 8:2 (p.160). *Cf. Megillah* 17b (end). We find that the Messiah will reveal himself on the Temple roof, *Yalkut* 2:499.

16. Rambam, Bertenoro, *Tosafot Yom Tov,* on *Sanhedrin* 1:3, Rambam on *Bekhorot* 4:3, *Yad, Sanhedrin* 4:11. For discussion, see Radbaz on *Yad, Sanhedrin* 4:11, *Tshuvot Ralbach, Kuntres HaSemichah, Tshuvot Yaakov BeRab* p. 199, *Bet Yosef, Choshen Mishpat* 295, *Birkey Yosef, Chosen Mishpat* 64, *Shach, Yoreh Deah* 242:22, *Sema, Choshen Mishpat 1:9, Minchat Chinukh* 491, Yaakov Emdin (Maharibatz), *Sanhedrin* 14a. In the year 5298 (1538 C.E.), Rabbi Yaakov Berab restored this ordination, granting it to four scholars, Rabbis Joseph Caro, Moshe di Trani, Joseph Sagis, and Moshe Cordevero, but it was later discontinued.
17. *Eruvin* 43b, Maharitz Chajot *ad loc., Kereiti U'Peleiti, Bet HaSafek,* end; Rashash, *Sanhedrin* 13b.
18. See commentaries *ad loc., Yalkut* 2:620, *Kuzari* 3:73 (77a).
19. Ezekiel 38, 39.
20. Zechariah 12:2, 14:2, Radak *ad loc., Yalkut* 2:578.
21. See *Succah* 52b, *BaMidbar Rabbah* 14:2, Radak on Zechariah 2:3; *Bereshit Rabbah* 99:2, 73:5, 75:6; *Bava Batra* 123b, on Obadiah 1:18; *Or HaChaim* on Numbers 24:17. Also see Isaiah 11:13, Ramban on Exodus 17:9 (end), Ezekiel 37:16, Rashi, Radak, Ibn Ezra, on Zechariah 12:10. See Chapter 7, note 32.
22. *Pirkey Rabbi Eliezer* 31 (72a).
23. Jeremiah 3:17, *Shemot Rabbah* 23:11, *Avot D'Rabbi Natan* 35:9.

EYE OF THE UNIVERSE

1. *Tanchuma, Kedoshim* 10, *Pesikta Rabatai* 10:2, *Zohar* 2:157a, 2:222b, Ramban on Genesis 14:18, *Shalshelet HaKaballah* p. 31, *Likutey Torah* (R. Shneur Zalman of Liadi) *Masai* 91b.
2. *Yoma* 5:2 (53b), *VaYikra Rabbah* 20:4, *Pesikta* 26 (171a), *Zohar* 1:71b (end), 1:231a, *Zohar Chadash* 28a; *Yad, Bet HaBechirah* 4:1, Rashi on Job 39:28. See *Likutey Moharan* 61:6, from Job 31:35.
3. *Tosefta, Yoma* 2:12; *Yoma* 54b, *Pirkey Rabbi Eliezer* 35 (82b), *Midrash Tehillim 91, Zohar* 1:131a, 1:86b, 87a, Ramban, Bachya, on Genesis 28:19. Also see *Zohar* 1:231a, 222a, *Tikuney Zohar* 67 (98a). God's Name is inscribed on this stone, see *Targum J.* on Exodus 28:39, Ecclesiastes 3:11.
4. *Bereshit Rabbah* 5:8. Creation began at a single point, *Bereshit Rabbah* 4:2.
5. *Moreh Nebukhim,* introduction to part 2, #16; *Or HaShem* 1:1:16, *ShefaTal* 1:3 (Hanau 5372) p. 13c in note, *Pardes Rimonim* 2:7, *Amud HaAvodah, Vikuach Shoel U'Meshiv* 99. See note 7. Also see "Tefillin" (NCSY, New York, 1973) p. 42. *Cf. Toledot Yaakov Yosef* 197c, *Tzafnat Paneach* 26d, 68d, *Sefer Baal Shem Tov, Ekev* 72, *Bereshit* 41.
6. *Bereshit Rabbah* 50:2, *Targum,* Rashi, on Genesis 18:2, *Zohar* 1:127a.
7. For a similar argument, see *Yad, Yesodey HaTorah* 1:7, 2:5, see Commentary *ad loc.*
8. *Shabbat* 89a, *Bereshit Rabbah* 48:11.
9. *Pitchey Chakhmah VaDaat* 4, *Shefa Tal* 3:1.
10. *Zohar* 3:90b.
11. It is thus written, "He makes peace in His high places" (Job 25:2), see Rashi *ad loc., Bereshit Rabbah* 12:8, *BaMidbar Rabbah* 12:8, *Bahir* 11, 59, 153. Also see *Chagigah* 12a, *Bereshit Rabbah* 4:7, Rashi on Genesis 1:8.
12. The word *Bereshyt* can thus be read as *Bara Shyt* — "He created the *Shyt*" — the *Shyt* being the foundation and drainage pit of the Altar, see *Succah* 49a. Note that *Shyt* is masculine, while *Shetiyah is* feminine, both words sharing the same root. The *Shetiyah* was the foundation of both the physical and spiritual worlds, see *Yoma* 54b. It was a place of constriction (*tzimtzum*) of spiritual forces, *cf. Likutey Moharan* 61:6.
13. *Bereshit Rabbah* 8:3. Note that the Jew was also created on the spot, since key events in the lives of the Patriarchs occurred here, see Chapter 6, notes 28, 45, 49.
14. *Avot Rabbi Natan* 31:3, Saadya Gaon on *Sefer Yetzirah* 4: 1, *Tikkuney Zohar* 17a.
15. *Cf. Metzudot David* (Radbaz) 266.
16. See Chapter 6, note 4.
17. Isaiah 59:2, Rambam, *Shemoneh Perakim* #8, *Reshit Chakhmah* 1:7 (22d), *Nefesh HaChaim* 1:18.
18. See Chapter 5, note 15.
19. See *Shabbat* 33a, 137b, *Pesachim* 68b, *Taanit* 27b, *Megillah* 31b, *Nedarim* 31b, *Avodah Zarah* 3a, *Tosefta, Berakhot* 6:18, *Yebamot* 2:6, Commentaries on *Avot* 1:2.
20. *Shabbat* 88a, Rashi on Genesis 1:31.
21. *Kohelet Rabbah* 2:7, *Tanchuma, Kedoshim* 10, Rashi on Ecclesiastes 2:5, *Sichot HaRan* 60.
22. *Tzioni ad loc., Sodey Razia* (Bilgorai 5696) p. 35a, *Megalah Amukot* 121, 128, 131, 134, 178.
23. *Taanit* 5a, Rashba (in *Eyin Yaakov*) *ad loc., Chagigah* 12b, *Tanchuma, Pekudey 1, Zohar* 1:80, 1:183a, 2:59a, Ramban on Genesis 14:18; *Yerushalmi, Berakhot* 4:5 (35b), Ibn Ezra on Psalms 76:3, Rashi on Genesis 28:17, *Targum,* Rashi, on Psalms 122:3.
24. *Zohar* 1:87a, 3:90b.
25. *Derekh HaShem* 2:5:4, 3:2:5
26. *Yad, Yesodey HaTorah* 2:9, *Moreh Nebukhim* 1:69, *Likutey Amarim* (Tanya), *Shaar Ha Yichud VeHaEmunah*
27. Deuteronomy 12:11, 14:23, 16:2, 16:6, 16:11, 26:2. See 1 Kings 8:29. Also see Chapter 6, note 1.
28. See *Sichot HaRan* 40.
29. Jerusalem is thus identified with *Yesod*-Foundation, the Attribute that unites Male and Female, see *Etz Chaim, Shaar HaArat HaMochin* 5 (p.126), *Shaar Kitzur ABYA* 1 (p. 393). *Cf. Zohar* 2:184b, *Mavo Shaarim* 4:2:7(p. 165), *Shaarey Gan Eden* 89a, *Siddur Rabbi Shneur Zalman of Liadi* p.53d, 59b, 62c, *Torah Or* 37d, *Likutey Torah, Ekev* (16c, d).
30. *Taanit* 5a. See *Pardes Rimonim* 8:26, *Shnei Luchot HaBrit, TorahSheBeKtav,* beginning of *VaYechi* (3:66b), *Likutey Torah* (R. Shneur Zalman), *Pekudey* (4a).
31. *Succah* 55b. Regarding these seventy directing angels, see *Targum J.* on Deuteronomy 32:8, Genesis 11:7, 8, *Pirkey Rabbi Eliezer* 24, Ibn Ezra on Zechariah 1:8, *Derekh HaShem* 2:4:8.
32. See Bachya on Deuteronomy 4:7, *Tshuvot Rivash* 157, *Elemah Rabatai, Eyin Kall* 1:2, *Pardes Rimonim* 32:2, *Metzudot David* (Radbaz) 2, *Shomer Emunim* (*HaKadmon*) 2:64, 65, *Kisey Melekh* (on *Tikuney Zohar* 22) 94b #50.
33. *Berakhot* 7a, *Otzar HaKavod ad loc., Siddur Rabbi Shneur Zalman of Liadi* p. 136c.
34. *Likutey Moharan* 26.
35. For details, see "The Jew," Collegiate Hashkafa Series, Young Israel, New York, 1973.
36. See note 31.
37. This was thus the place of the creation of Adam, the father of the entire human race.

FOCUS OF A PEOPLE

1. *Sefer HaChinukh* 487. See Chapter 6, note 1.
2. According to traditions, David captured Jerusalem in the year 2892 (868 B.C.E), and it was destroyed by the Romans in 3828 (69 C.E.), or 976 years later. See Chapter 7, notes 22 and 53. According to Josephus, however, Jerusalem retained this status for 1179 years, see *Wars* 6:10. Also see *Antiquities* 20:10.
3. *Kelim* 1:8. *Cf. Bava Kama* 62b, *Yad, Bet HaBechirah* 7:14. Also see *Ketubot* 13:11 (110b), Isaiah 52:1, 66:20.
4. *Yerushalmi, Chagigah* 3:6, *Bava Kama* 7:7, from Psalms 122:3. Cf. *Chagigah* 26a, Isaiah 33:20.
5. *Ibid.* Cf. *Metzudot David* (Radbaz) 266.
6. Hirsch on Genesis 4:17. Note that Cain was originally a farmer, and that the first city was built by Cain as an atonement for his murder of his brother. *Cf. Malbim ibid.* Their *altar* was in Jerusalem, see Chapter 6, note 9.
7. See Genesis 4:20-22.
8. *Ketubot* 111b, from 2 Kings 19:34; *Tanchuma, Ki Tavo* 4, from Lamentations 2:15. *Cf. Likutey Moharan* 280.
9. This was the tithe given annually, except for the fourth and sixth year of the seven-year cycle, when the Tithe for the Poor (*Maaser Ani*) was substituted as a second tithe. See *Yad, Matnot Aniyim* 6, *Maaser Sheni* 1:1.
10. Hirsch on Deuteronomy 14:23.
11. Deuteronomy 14:23, Ibn Ezra, Rashbam, Sforno *ad loc., Tosafot, Bava Batra* 21a, s.v. "*Ki.*" See *Chinukh* 360, *Metzudot David* 256.
12. *Chinukh* 360.
13. Deuteronomy 26:2. See *Bikkurim* 3:1-4.
14. Ramban on Leviticus 1:9. See *Tanchuma, VaYikra* 8.
15. *Chinukh* 95.
16. Man is thus like an angel in three ways, and like an animal in three ways, *Chagigah* 16a. Also see *Tanchuma, VaYikra* 8, *Zohar* 2:94b, 3:33b, Ramban on *Genesis* 1:20, Leviticus 17:24, Ralbag on Proverbs 12:10, *Shaarey Kedushah* 1:1, *Or HaChaim* on *Genesis* 1:21, Leviticus17:10, *Likutey Amarim* (*Tanya*) 1:1 (5b).
17. *Etz Chaim, Shaar Kitzur ABYA* 2 (Aslag edition, Tel Aviv, 5720), Volume 2, page 395. *Cf.* Ramban on Genesis 2:8, 3:22.
18. *Cf. Yoma* 9b, 39b, *Tosefta, Minachot* 13:4, *Yerushalmi, Yoma* 1:1 (4b), *BaMidbar Rabbah* 7:10. Also see Isaiah 1:11, Jeremiah 7:11, Psalms 50:12.
19. *Yad, Maaseh Karbanot* 18:2.
20. *Chinukh* 186.
21. *Yad, Maaseh Karbanot* 18:1, *Chinukh* 453.

22. Leviticus 1:4, 3:2, 3:8, 3:13, 4:4, 4:24, 4:29, 4:33, 16:21; *Minachot* 93b, *Yad, Maaseh Karbanot* 3:6, 8.
23. *Yoma* 86b, *Shemot Rabbah* 38:4, *Pesikta* 6 (60b), *Yalkut* 2:479. Also see *Minachot* 110a, *Taanit* 27a, *Megillah* 31a; *Rosh, Rosh HaShanah* 4:14, *Orach Chaim* 1:5.
24. *Chinukh 95, Yad, Bet HaBechirah* 6:16.

THE TEMPLE

1. See Chapter 7, note 53.
2. Some say that the commandment to build the Tabernacle was given after the sin of the Golden Calf, see Rashi on Exodus 31:18, 33:11, *Tanchuma, Terumah* 8, *Pekudey* 11. Others, however, maintain that it was before the Golden Calf, see *Baaley Tosafot*, Ramban, Ibn Ezra, on Exodus 25:1, *Midrash Lekach Tov, Ki Tisa* 105a, *Tana DeBei Eliahu Rabbah* 17. Also see Josephus, *Antiquities* 3:5:8.
3. *Seder Olam Rabbah* 6; *Zohar* 1:129a in *Midrash Ne'elam.*
4. *Tanchuma, Pekudey* 2, *Zohar* 2: 162b.
5. *Berakhot* 55a, *Zohar* 2:152a, 3:324b, Ramban on Exodus 31:2.
6. *Yad, Bet HaBechirah* 1:2, *Seder Olam Rabbah* 11. See *Zevachim* 14:5-8, *Tosefot Yom Tov, Tiferet Yisrael, ad loc.* Regarding Gilgal, see Joshua 5:9, Shiloh, Joshua 18:1, Nob, 1 Samuel 21:2, Gibeon, 1 Kings 3:4, Chapter 7, note 28.
7. *Yad, Melachim* 1:1, *Lechem Mishnah ad loc.*
8. Rashi *ad loc.* Note that a king is to be appointed when "you dwell in the land" (Deuteronomy 17:14), while the Temple is to be built "when you dwell in the land ... and He gives you rest." See Chapter 7, note 32, Chapter 8, note 21.
9. *Orach Chaim* 660:1, *Teshuvot Chatam Sofer, Orach Chaim* 28. See *Succah* 51b, *Yad, Tefillah* 11:3, *Orach Chaim* 150:5 in *Hagah.*
10. Ramban on Exodus 27:20, *Sifra* on Leviticus 24:2, *Sifri* on Numbers 8:2, *Teshuvot Rashba* 1:79. See *Yad, Bet HaBechirah* 3:8.
11. Exodus 25:11-30, 30:1-10, 37:17-28, 40:22-27; *Yad, Bet HaBechirah* 3:17.
12. This is described in Leviticus 16, and the entire tract of *Yoma* is a description of this service.
13. Exodus 25:10, 17, 40:18. See *Likutey Moharan* 2:6.
14. Deuteronomy 31:26, Rashi ad loc.; *Bava Batra* 14a. See Radak, Ralbag, Abarbanel on 1 Kings 8:9.
15. *Shekalim* 6:2, *Tiferet Yisrael ad loc., Yad, Bet HaBechirah* 4: 1. See *Yoma* 52b, *Horiot* 12a, *Keritot* 5b; *Tosefta Yoma* 2:13, *Tosefta Sotah* 13:2, *Yerushalmi Shekalim* 6:1 (24b), *Seder Olam Rabbah* 24, *Yalkut* 2:247; *Kuzari* 3:39 (48b); Rashi, Radak, Ralbag, on 2 Chronicles 35:3. For a discussion whether the Ark was concealed or carried off to Babylon, see *Yoma* 53b. There is a debate in *Yoma* 54a as to whether it was hidden under the Holy of Holies or in the Chamber of the Woodshed.
16. Deuteronomy 9:9, 11, 15.
17. Exodus 31:18, 34:29. See Bachya on Exodus 31:18.
18. *Yad, Sefer Torah* 10:11.
19. Actually, the curtains of the Holy of Holies may have been opened during the annual pilgrimages so that the people would be able to see the Ark.

    See *Yoma* 54a, *Tosafot Yeshenim ad loc., s.v. "U'Marin."* They thus actually may have seen the Ark and Cherubim of Moses, see Ritva *ibid.*
20. *Shemot Rabbah* 2:2, *Midrash Tehillim* 11:3. This seems to be disputed by the saying in *Rosh HaShanah* 31b, from Amos 7:7. The Midrash, however, apparently assumes that only seven of these steps actually occurred, and that the *Shekhinah* remained on the Western Wall. See Chapter 5, note 22.

THE SANHEDRIN

1. *Berakhot* 63b.
2. *Middot* 5:4, *Yoma* 19a, *Yad, Bet HaBechirah* 5:17. In *Middot*, the reading is that the *Lishkat HaGazit* was to the south, but according to most authorities, the correct reading is that it was to the north. See *Tosafot Yom Tov ad loc., Tosafot Yeshenim, Yoma, loc. cit.* Also see *Peah* 2:6, *Sanhedrin* 11:2 (86b).
3. *Sanhedrin* 16b, *Yad, Sanhedrin* 1:1, *Chinukh* 491.
4. *Sanhedrin* 1:6 (2a), *Yad, Sanhedrin* 1:3. *Cf. VaYikra Rabbah* 33:2, *Eikhah Rabbah,* introduction:24.
5. The only place where *Ohel Moed* has a different meaning is in Exodus 33:7 (see Rashi *ad loc.*), but there it is rendered by the Targum as Mishkan *Bet Ulfana,* meaning "Tabernacle of teaching." Usually, however, *Ohel Moed* is rendered by the Targum as *Mishkan Zimna;* in such cases, it refers to the Tabernacle, as, for example in Exodus 27:21. The verse used here from Numbers is also rendered *Mishkan Zimna.*
6. *Yerushalmi, Makkot* 2:6, *Mekhilta* on Exodus 20:23, 21:14, Rashi on Exodus 21:1; *Tosafot, Avodah Zarah* 8b, s.v. *"Melamed." Cf. Sanhedrin* 7b.
7. *Yad, Sanhedrin* 2:7, *Choshen Mishpat* 7:11. *Cf. Sanhedrin* 88b, *Yerushalmi, Sanhedrin* 1:4 (8b), *Tosefta, Chagigah* 2:4, *Devarim Rabbah* 1:7.
8. During the persecutions of Constantine (337-361 C.E.), the Sanhedrin had to go into hiding, and soon after this it was disbanded. See Ramban on *Sefer HaMitzvot, Mitzvah Aseh* 153. Also see *Bava Metzia* 86a, *Bereshit Rabbah* 31:12, *Yad,* Introduction.
9. *Sanhedrin* 88b, *Tosefta Sanhedrin* 7:1, *Tosefta Chagigah 2:4, Yerushalmi Sanhedrin* 1:4 (8b), *Yad, Sanhedrin* 2:8, *Mamrim* 1:4.
10. *Sifri* on Deuteronomy 17:11, *Yad, Mamrim* 1:2, *Berakhot* 6:2, 11:3, *Chinukh* 496, Maharitz Chajot, *Succah* 46a; Ramban on *Sefer HaMitzvot, Shoresh 2* (27b).
11. *Yad, Mamrim* 1:1.
12. *Sifri,* Rashi *ad loc., Chulin* 28a, *Yoma* 75b, *Yad, Shechitah* 1:4. *Cf. Tana DeBei Eliahu Rabbah* 15 (74a).
13. See Deuteronomy 6:8, Numbers 15:38; *Chagigah* 1:8 (10a), *Mekhilta* on Exodus 35:1, *Shabbat* 97b (top), *Yerushalmi, Shabbat* 7:2 (44a), *VaYikra Rabbah 22:1, Kohelet Rabbah 5:7.* Also see *Sanhedrin* 88b, *Kuzari* 3:35(39a), Raavad on *Sifra,* introduction (la); *Shabbat* 31a.
14. *Yerushalmi, Peah* 2:4 (13a), *Chagigah* 1:8 (7b), *Megillah* 4:1 (28a); *BaMidbar Rabbah* 14:12, *Shir HaShirim Rabbah* 1:18.
15. *Gittin* 61b, *Tanchuma, Noah* 3.
16. Kuzari 3:39 (46a).
17. *Sifri,* Rashi, *ad loc., Sanhedrin* 87a, Rashi on Joshua 15:3, Psalms 132:6.
18. *Zevachim* 55b, *Sifri* on Deuteronomy 33:12.
19. *Kuzari* 3:38 (42b), Ramban on *Megillah* 2a; Rashi, *Yebamot* 13b s.v. *"Lo."*
20. *Yoma* 25a.
21. *Berakhot* 9:5 (54a).
22. *Yoma* 25a. See commentaries on Psalms 52:16. This was an important task of the Sanhedrin, see *Middot* 5:4, *Yad, Biyat HaMikdash* 6:11.
23. *Yad, Biyat HaMikdash* 2:5, *Chinukh* 151, from Leviticus 10:7, 21:2.
24. *Mekhilta* on Exodus 20:23 and 21:14. Both derivations are required; one teaches that they should be in proximity to one another, while the other teaches that there should be direct access from one to the other. See note 6.
25. *Bava Batra* 25b, *Orach Chaim* 94:2 in *Hagah.*
26. *Pardes Rimonim* 23:18, s.v. *"Tzafon."*
27. *Zevachim* 54a, *Yad, Bet HaBechirah* 1:14. *Cf.* 1 Kings 6:7.
28. Bachya on Exodus 20:22.
29. See Hirsch on Exodus 20:22. *Cf.* Ritva, *Yoma* 19a; *Arukh, s.v. "Gazit."* Others, however, define *Gazit* differently, see *Arukh loc. cit.,* from Numbers 11:31. See 1 Kings 5:31, 6:36, 7:9, 7:11, Isaiah 9:9, Ezekiel 40:42, Amos 5:11, Lamentations 3:9, 1 Chronicles 22:2. Note that the Tablets were also made of cut stone, see Exodus 34:1.
30. *Yerushalmi, Horiot* 1:1; *Avodah Zarah* 8b; *Sifri,* Hirsch on Deuteronomy 17:10.
31. *Tamid* 4:3 (end), Bertenoro, *Tiferet Yisrael* (63) *ad loc., Yad, Temidim U'Musafim* 6:4. *Cf. Beer Sheva, Tamid* 31b.
32. *Berakhot* 8a, *Megillah* 28a, *Yad, Tefillah* 8:3, *Orach Chaim* 90:18. While worshiping there, they also faced the south, the direction of wisdom, see note 25.
33. *Bereshit Rabbah* 55:7. See *Taanit* 16a, *Yerushalmi, Berakhot* 4:5 (35b).
34. See *Chinukh* 404*;* Ibn Ezra, Sforno, on Deuteronomy 14:23. *Cf. Yerushalmi Megillah* 3:1 (23a), *Ketubot* 13:1 (67b), *Shir HaShirim Rabbah* 5:10, *Eikha Rabbah,* Introduction: 12.

KINGS AND PROPHETS

1. Tosefta, Sanhedrin 3:2; *Sifri,* Ramban, on Deuteronomy 17:5; *Yad, Sanhedrin 5:1, Melakhim* 1:3.
2. Deuteronomy 17:18, 19; *Sanhedrin* 21a, *Yad, Melakhim* 3:1.
3. See Maharitz Chajot, *Torat Nevi'im* 7, for discussion regarding this.
4. *Sanhedrin* 1:5 (2a), *Shavuot* 2:2 (14a), *Yad, Bet HaBechirah* 6:11 (from Exodus 25:8, 9), *Sanhedrin* 5:1. See *Sifri,* Ramban, on Deuteronomy 12:5, from 2 Samuel 24:18. This is particularly true of the initial dedication of Jerusalem, see *Yerushalmi, Sanhedrin* 1:3, from 2 Chronicles 3:1, *Yad, Bet HaBechirah* 6:14. See *Bava Batra* 4a.
5. Radak on 2 Samuel 5:6, Psalms 2:6.
6. In this respect, the king was very much like a sacred vessel, which was sanctified through its prescribed use, *cf. Yad, Kli HaMikdash* 1:12. A

king was anointed in a similar manner, *ibid.* 1:11. Regarding the anointing of priests, see *ibid.* 4:13. See Deuteronomy 17:20, *Horiot* 11b.

7. See *Tanchuma, Kedoshim* 1, *Zohar* 3:78a. There are other allusions in the Torah that the Royal Palace should be in Jerusalem. First, the reading describing the king follows directly after that prescribing that the Sanhedrin should be in Jerusalem. Second, the king is said to rule forever "in the midst of Israel" (Deuteronomy 17:20), and Jerusalem is said to be central to the Jewish people. Furthermore, in the entire Book of Deuteronomy, the expression stating that God "will choose" (*YiBh'char*) only occurs in reference to Jerusalem, and in this one case, to the king. Also see Deuteronomy 33:5, Bachya on Deuteronomy 17:14.
8. See *Yad,* Introduction.
9. *Megillah* 15a, *Eikha Rabbah,* Introduction:24.
10. Rashi, *Taanit* 16a *"Horah," Agadat Bereshit* 14:3, *Targum Sheni* on Esther 4:1, *Torah Temimah,* Genesis 22:5. Samuel thus had his first prophecy near the sanctuary, see 1 Samuel 3:3, commentaries *ad loc. Cf.* Isaiah 6:1. Abraham's vision described in Genesis 15 also occurred directly after he met with Malchitzedek, king of Jerusalem, and also may have been in proximity to the Holy City.
11. *Shabbat* 92a, *Nedarim* 38a, *Yad, Yesodey HaTorah* 7:1, *Moreh Nebukhim* 2:36, Ramban on *Avot* 4:1, *Shemonah Perakim #7, Iggeret Temon* (Warsaw 5686) p. 31, *Tshuvot Rashba* 1:548.
12. *Yad,* Introduction. See *Megillah* 17b, Ramban on *Sefer HaMitzvot, Shoresh* 2 (27b); *Shabbat* 14b, *Succah* 44a, *Bava Kama* 82a; *Tosafot, Bava Batra* 147a, s.v. *"Menayin,"* Rashash, *Megillah* 14a, *Kuzari* 3:41 (50a), Rash, Bertenoro on *Yadayim* 4:3, s.v. *"Maaseh," Mishnah LaMelekh* on *Yad, Megillah* 1:11.
13. Hai Gaon, in *Tshuvot HaGaonim* (*Shaarey Tshuvah*) #14.
14. *Turey Aven* on *Yad, Yesodey HaTorah* 10:2, from *Yebamot* 64b. Moses was accordingly given three signs, Exodus 4:9.
15. *Yad, Yesodey HaTorah* 10:1. *Cf. Sotah* 12b.
16. *Sanhedrin* 1:5 (2a), *Yad, Sanhedrin* 5:1. See *Tshuvot HaGaonim loc. cit.*
17. Exodus 3:16, 4:29. See *Mekhilta,* Ramban, on Exodus 12:21.
18. *Bava Batra* 15a.
19. *Derashot HaRan* #8 (Jerusalem 5734) p. 128; *Avodat HaKodesh* 4:25. See *Bereshit Rabbah* 70:8. Before the Temple was built and the Ark stood in its proper place, prophecy was therefore difficult to attain, see 1 Samuel 3:1.
20. See Numbers 7:89.
21. Abarbanel on 1 Samuel 3:3. This may be why God was said to "dwell among the Cherubim" (1 Samuel 4:4, 2 Samuel 6:2), and to "ride on a Cherub," Psalms 18:11, see *Targum ad loc.*
22. *Succah* 5b, *Chagigah* 13b; Rashi, Rashbam, Ibn Ezra, on Exodus 25:18.
23. *Mekhilta* on Exodus 20:20.
24. *Moreh Nebukhim* 3:45, *Chizkuni* on Exodus 25:18.
25. The Cherubim are therefore seen as the angels of Gehenom, through which one must pass before he enters Paradise, see *Targum J.,* Bachya, on Genesis 3:24. The "Tree of Life" also is said to refer to the Torah (Proverbs 3:18), and the Cherubim thus "guarded" the original Torah that stood in the Ark.
26. Radak, Abarbanel, on Ezekiel 1:28; *Devarim Rabbah* 7:8, Rashi, *Chagigah* 13b *"Ra'ah."*
27. Ezekiel 1:5, 10:20; *Chagigah* 13b.
28. The Cherubim on the Ark are thus called the *Markava,* see 1 Chronicles 28:18, commentaries *ad loc.* Regarding the meaning of the *Markava* in general, see commentaries on *Chagigah* 2:1, *Hekhelot Rabatai* 1:1; R. Chananel, Hai Gaon (quoted in *HaKotev* in *Eyin Yaakov*) on *Chagigah*14b.
29. See *Midrash HaGadol,* Ramban, Bachya, *Tzioni,* Hirsch, on Exodus 25:18, *Tanchuma VaYakhel* 7, *Moreh Nebukhim* 3:45, *Zohar* 1:32b.
30. *Berakhot* 8a, from Psalms 87:2. Zion thus refers to Jerusalem, but primarily to the place of the Sanhedrin. Also see Isaiah 33:20, *Pesikta Rabatai* 41. The Temple Mount is called Zion, 1 Kings 8:1, Isaiah 1:27. Zion is also in the portion of Judah, the part of the Temple Mount where the Sanhedrin sat, Psalms 78:67. *Cf.* 2 Samuel 5:7.

THE GATE OF PRAYER

1. See 1 Kings 8:29, 30, 33, 35, 38, 42, 44, 48; 2 Chronicles 6:21 *ff.*
2. Daniel 6:11. See *Tosefta, Berakhot* 3:8.
3. Ramban *ad loc., Pirkey Rabbi Eliezer* 35 (82b). *Cf.* Ibn Ezra on Psalms 76:3, Radak on 2 Samuel 24:16, *Metzudot David* (Radbaz) 304. Also see *Kuzari* 2:14 (17b), *Zohar* 1:150b, 2:79a. Regarding Jacob, see below, Chapter 6, note 45.
4. See Radal on *Pirkey Rabbi Eliezer* 35:63.
5. *Berakhot* 30a, *Tosefta, Berakhot* 3:16.
6. *Tur, Orach Chaim* 98.
7. R. Yonah on *Berakhot,* Rif 22b *"Tzarikh."*
8. *Shulchan Arukh, Orach Chaim* 98:1.
9. *Berakhot* 4:5 (28b).
10. *Perishah on Tur, Orach Chaim* 94:1.
11. See Chapter 1, note 23.
12. *Berakhot* 26b; *Yad, Tefillah* 1:5.
13. *Tur, Orach Chaim* 98.
14. *Noam HaMitzvot* 440. In the Temple itself, one would never turn his back to the Holy of Holies. Therefore, all sacrifices were offered with the priest facing this direction. See *Yoma* 53a, *Yad, Bet HaBechirah* 7:4, *Tosafot, Yoma* 25a, s.v. *"Hah." Cf.* Ezekiel 8:16.
15. *Bahir* (Ed. Margolies, Jerusalem 5711) #123. See *Avodat HaKodesh* 1:6, 2:14. Also see *Bahir* 109, *Zohar* 3:9a, 1:89b, Ramban on Genesis 2:8.
16. See *Berakhot* 31a, *Zohar* 1:202b, 3:8b, Radak on Psalms 135:21, *Likutey Moharan* 1:1.
17. *Berakhot* 49a, *Midrash Tehillim* 121:3, *Shir HaShirim Rabbah* 4.
18. *Yad, Bet HaBechirah* 6:16.
19. *Kaftor Va'Pherach* 6 (15a), Radbaz 691, *Magen Avraham* 561:2, *Tshuvot Chatam Sofer, Yoreh Deah* 233, 234. Others, however, dispute this and maintain that there is no penalty today, Raavad, *Bet HaBechirah* 6:15. *Cf. Zevachim* 107b, *Tosafot, Shabbat* 14b, s.v. *"VeNe'elam."*
20. *Rashi ad loc., VaYikra Rabbah* 24:4.
21. *Zohar* 3:36, 3:74, *Likutey Torah* (R. Shneur Zalman of Liadi), *Masai* 91b.
22. *Metzudot David* (Radbaz) 418. See Chapter 2, note 20.